BALD EAGLE

NATIONAL GEOGRAPHIC KIDS™

BIRD GUIDE
OF NORTH AMERICA

THE BEST BIRDING BOOK FOR KIDS FROM NATIONAL GEOGRAPHIC'S BIRD EXPERTS

BY JONATHAN ALDERFER

NATIONAL
GEOGRAPHIC

WASHINGTON, D.C.

Contents

Anna's Hummingbird

Osprey

Great Blue Heron

Greater Roadrunner

BIRDS ARE BEAUTIFUL
AND AWE-INSPIRING WILD ANIMALS THAT LIVE EVERYWHERE WE DO.

Many people get so interested in birds that they become bird-watchers (also called birders). They like to learn about birds so that they can identify the birds they see, or just to be entertained. Did you know that bird-watching is one of the most popular hobbies in North America? About 44 million people watch birds, just in the United States. There's a good chance that someone in your family could be a bird-watcher.

But, bird-watching isn't just for grown-ups. Lots of kids are bird-watchers, too. A great way to get started is to put up a feeder so you can watch birds in your backyard—check out the simple plan to make your own bird feeder in the back of this book. It's easy to get hooked on birds, and soon you'll want to look for birds beyond your backyard.

Bird-watching, it's like going on a treasure hunt—keep your eyes and ears open and you might just find something really cool. Keep a list of what you see, and add to your collection of bird sightings throughout the year.

Join me on a tour of the 100 bird species in this book. You'll find all kinds of birds inside, from huge predators, like the Bald Eagle, to tiny hummingbirds, and everything in between. All the birds are divided into ten different habitats—like deserts, prairies, and even backyards. Look for a habitat that matches where you live. That's a good place to start. And, welcome to the club!

—Jonathan Alderfer

ROSEATE SPOONBILL

How to Use This Book!

FORTY BIRDS ARE PROFILED THROUGHOUT THIS BOOK, WITH AN ADDITIONAL 60 BIRDS INTRODUCED IN MINI-PROFILES AT THE END OF EACH SECTION.

THE TITLE CLEARLY SHOWS YOU WHICH HABITAT YOU WILL READ ABOUT.

EACH SECTION IS COLOR-CODED WITH A TAB TO HELP YOU KEEP TRACK OF WHAT SECTION YOU ARE IN.

Western
Backyard
Birds

ANNA'S HUMMINGBIRD

TO FIND OUT THE NAME OF THE BIRD SHOWN ON EACH OPENER, LOOK FOR EACH BIRD'S COMMON NAME.

THE PHOTOS ON THE HABITAT SPREADS ILLUSTRATE AN EXAMPLE OF WHAT EACH HABITAT LOOKS LIKE.

THE TEN BIRDS YOU WILL READ ABOUT IN EACH SECTION ARE INTRODUCED ON THESE SPREADS. PHOTOS OF THE BIRDS ARE PLACED IN LOCATIONS WHERE YOU ARE LIKELY TO SEE THEM WHEN BIRD-WATCHING.

Southern Swamp and Bayou
HABITAT

SWALLOW-TAILED KITE

BARRED OWL

PILEATED WOODPECKER

YELLOW-CROWNED NIGHT-HERON

ANHINGA

PURPLE GALLINULE

PROTHONOTARY WARBLER

SNOWY EGRET

WOOD DUCK

LIMPKIN

A UNIQUE PLACE TO LIVE

A swamp is a low-lying wooded area that is usually flooded with overflow from a nearby river or lake, and is full of plant and animal life. Tupelo, cypress, and other types of trees and vegetation get lots of water and nutrients. Bayou, found along the Gulf Coast, can be a slow-moving river or stream, or a marshy lake or wetland. Many types of animals—crayfish, shrimp, catfish, alligators, frogs, and a great variety of insects—are abundant in a swamp or bayou, and so are the birds that feed on them.

INTRODUCTORY TEXT PROVIDES BASIC INFORMATION ABOUT EACH HABITAT.

YOU WILL FIND EACH BIRD'S COMMON NAME IN THE UPPER LEFT CORNER OF EACH PROFILE SPREAD.

FIND OUT THE DIFFERENT TYPES OF SOUNDS BIRDS MAKE IN THIS SECTION.

BIRDS HAVE A VARIED DIET. FIND OUT WHAT TYPES OF FOOD EACH SPECIES EATS IN THIS SECTION.

THE YELLOW BOXES INCLUDE FUN FACTS ABOUT EACH SPECIES.

THIS SECTION POINTS OUT DIFFERENT BODY PARTS AND, IN MANY CASES, THE PURPOSE OF EACH.

THE MAP SHOWS EACH BIRD'S RANGE WITH DIFFERENT COLORS. THE KEY EXPLAINS WHAT EACH COLOR ON THE MAP ILLUSTRATES.

THE FACT BOX PROVIDES FAST FACTS ABOUT EACH SPECIES, INCLUDING ITS SCIENTIFIC NAME, LENGTH, AND WINGSPAN.

THE PLACES AND TYPES OF ENVIRONMENTS IN WHICH THEY LIVE CAN BE FOUND HERE.

THE SIDEBAR PROVIDES MORE INFORMATION ABOUT EACH SPECIES, INCLUDING INFORMATION ABOUT BEHAVIOR, BABIES, BUILDING NESTS, AND MUCH MORE.

THE INTRODUCTORY TEXT WILL INTRODUCE YOU TO THE SPECIES, PROVIDING BASIC INFORMATION ABOUT IT.

THE TITLE OF EACH OF THESE SPREADS IS LOCATED IN THE UPPER LEFT CORNER.

TEXT BLOCKS NEXT TO THE TITLE INTRODUCE THE GROUP OF BIRDS YOU WILL READ ABOUT.

THE TEXT BLOCKS THAT ACCOMPANY EACH BIRD PHOTO PROVIDE A BRIEF EXPLANATION OF EACH SPECIES.

FOR FAST FACTS ABOUT EACH SPECIES FOUND ON THESE SPREADS, CHECK OUT THE FACT BOXES. HERE YOU WILL FIND THE SCIENTIFIC NAME, LENGTH, AND WINGSPAN FOR EACH BIRD.

Mini-Profiles
EASTERN BACKYARD

Here are a few more of the many birds that live in eastern backyards. All of these birds—except the hawk—love to eat seeds from a bird feeder or scattered on the ground.

RED-SHOULDERED HAWK
Buteo lineatus

The colorful Red-shouldered Hawk is a very vocal bird with a loud screaming call, KEE-ahh. When you hear its call, look up to see it soaring over wooded backyards. To catch its prey, the hawk perches quietly at the edge of the woods and then pounces down on small mammals and reptiles.

MOURNING DOVE
Zenaida macroura

There are the same number of Mourning Doves living in the U.S. as there are people—about 350 million. They live in open areas including suburban yards. Listen for the dove's slow, mournful call, oowoo-woo-woo-woo, and the whistling sound made by its wings when it bursts into flight. You can attract doves to your backyard by scattering birdseed on the ground.

BLACK-CAPPED CHICKADEE
Poecile atricapillus

Chickadees are cute little birds that aren't very afraid of people and that love to come to bird feeders. The Black-capped and Carolina Chickadees are almost identical (black cap and throat, white cheek, and gray back), but the Black-capped lives in northern areas, while the Carolina lives in the southern U.S. The chickadee is named for its call: chick-a-dee-dee-dee.

WHITE-BREASTED NUTHATCH
Sitta carolinensis

If you see a small gray-and-white bird climbing nimbly up, down, and around a tree trunk, chances are good that you've spotted a white-breasted Nuthatch. The nuthatch has an extra-long hind claw that helps it get a grip in any position. It lives year-round in woods and wooded backyards and is crazy about suet feeders. Its call is a low pitched nasal yonk.

WHITE-THROATED SPARROW
Zonotrichia albicollis

In the spring, these sparrows travel to northern areas to breed, but in the winter they are very common around backyards and forest edges. Feed them by scattering seed on the ground and you might get a large flock hanging around all winter. Take a close look and you'll see that some sparrows have black-and-white head stripes (the hard-core aggressive birds) and others have tan-and-white stripes (the laid-back passive birds). This has nothing to do with being male or female, and successful breeding pairs usually consist of one of each type. Its song sounds like "Old Sam Peabody, Peabody, Peabody."

AMERICAN GOLDFINCH
Spinus tristis

From spring to fall, male goldfinches have dazzling yellow plumage and a black cap and wings. In the winter they are a more subdued tan color. Goldfinches are common in overgrown fields and along roadsides across the U.S., and they like to visit bird feeders. The goldfinch is the state bird of Iowa, New Jersey, and Washington. Its per-chik-o-ree sounds like laughter.

PEREGRINE FALCON

RUSSIA

ARCTIC OCEAN

165°
150°
135°
126°
105°
90°
75°
60°
30°
15°
45°
75°

ALASKA
(UNITED STATES)

Greenland
DENMARK

ARCTIC
CIRCLE

YUKON

NORTHWEST TERRITORIES

N U N A V U T

60°

BRITISH
COLUMBIA

ALBERTA

SASK.

MANITOBA

C A N A D A

NEWFOUNDLAND AND LABRADOR

QUEBEC

ONTARIO

45°

WASH.

MONTANA

NORTH
DAKOTA

MINN.

MICHIGAN

N.B. P.E.I.

ME.

NOVA SCOTIA

OREGON

IDAHO

WYOMING

SOUTH
DAKOTA

WIS.

VT.

N.H.

N.Y.

NEW HAMPSHIRE

MASSACHUSETTS

RHODE ISLAND

CONNECTICUT

DELAWARE

NEVADA

UTAH

COLORADO

NEBRASKA

IOWA

ILL.

IND.

OHIO

PA.

N.J.

MD.

CALIFORNIA

U N I T E D   S T A T E S

MO.

W.
VA.

VA.

ARIZONA

NEW
MEXICO

KANSAS

OKLA.

ARK.

KY.

TENN.

N.C.

S.C.

ATLANTIC

OCEAN

30°

TEXAS

LA.

MISS.

ALA.

GA.

FLORIDA

BAHAMAS

TROPIC OF CANCER

M E X I C O

W e s t   I n d i e s

C U B A

HAITI

PACIFIC

OCEAN

JAMAICA

DOMINICAN
REPUBLIC

15°

BELIZE

GUATEMALA

HONDURAS

EL SALVADOR

NICARAGUA

Azimuthal Equidistant Projection

0   400   800 MILES

0   400   800 KILOMETERS

COSTA RICA

PANAMA

SOUTH AMERICA

75°

EQUATOR

105°

90°

Map of North America

ABBREVIATIONS

Ala.	Alabama	N.J.	New Jersey
Ark.	Arkansas	N.Y.	New York
Ga.	Georgia	Okla.	Oklahoma
Ill.	Illinois	Pa.	Pennsylvania
Ind.	Indiana	P.E.I.	Prince Edward Island
Ky.	Kentucky	Sask.	Saskatchewan
La.	Louisiana	S.C.	South Carolina
Md.	Maryland	Tenn.	Tennessee
Me.	Maine	Va.	Virginia
Minn.	Minnesota	Vt.	Vermont
Miss.	Mississippi	Wash.	Washington
Mo.	Missouri	Wis.	Wisconsin
N.B.	New Brunswick	W. Va.	West Virginia
N.C.	North Carolina		

RANGE MAPS

The following is a sample of the range maps and map keys you will find on the bird profile pages throughout this book.

RANGE MAP KEY

- SUMMER (breeding)
- WINTER (nonbreeding)
- MIGRATION
- YEAR-ROUND

SAMPLE RANGE MAP

SUMMER (breeding)

MIGRATION

WINTER (nonbreeding)

YEAR-ROUND

Range Map of the Peregrine Falcon

Getting Started as a Birder

Common Grackle

Most kids are interested in nature and love to explore. You are one of those nature-loving kids if you are reading this book—that's a no-brainer. If you are wondering how to start exploring the world of birds living around you, this book will help.

WHERE ARE THE BIRDS?

HABITAT

Birds have favorite places, just like people. Although some birds seem to live just about everywhere, most birds prefer a specific type of place—or habitat. That's because the habitat—the land and plants of an area—provides them with what they need to live a healthy life. All of the birds described in this book are divided into ten different habitats because habitat is a great clue to what types of bird you might see in a particular area. For instance, sandpipers are found on mudflats and beaches, not up in trees with wood-peckers. Duh.

Many species—especially smaller birds—don't move around too much. The same chickadees that come to your feeder in fall and winter probably nest nearby in the summer. But birds have wings and can fly long distances. Some birds, like hawks and vultures, might fly many miles every day searching for food. Other birds migrate long distances, but once they get to where they want to nest or to spend the winter, most of them stay put for months.

"BIRDY" PLACES

Even within a specific habitat, there are places that are especially attractive to birds: places that have lots of food or that are safe to nest or to roost overnight. If you want to see lots of birds, be on the lookout for these special locations:

• **Edges.** Anywhere the habitat changes from one type to another, such as the place where a forest stops and a field begins.

• **Sheltered Areas.** Birds are attracted to small areas out of the wind because they tend to be warmer, especially in winter.

• **Water.** Water is a magnet for all kinds of birds in all kinds of places, from deserts to mountains.

• **Your Backyard.** A backyard or common area where you can put up a bird feeder and birdbath is likely to attract a large number of birds. There are plans in the back of this book that show you how to make your own.

WHAT BIRD IS IT?

BE A BIRD DETECTIVE

Once you are watching a bird, it's time to play detective. Each bird you see is a mystery for you to solve. And like any detective, you have to search for clues and gather evidence to help you solve each mystery. You can watch and identify birds without binoculars, but you'll get a much better look at the bird by using binoculars.

WHAT ARE ITS FIELD MARKS?

"Field mark" is the term that bird-watchers use to describe something unique about a particular species of bird. Field marks are the clues that will help you put a name to a mystery bird. The first thing that most people notice about a bird is its color, but there are a lot of other field marks. Sometimes you need only one clue to identify a mystery bird, but often you need several clues to find the answer. Here's a list of the most important types of field marks to consider:

- **Color**
- **Size**
- **Shape**
- **Behavior**
- **Song**

WHAT COLOR IS THE BIRD?

There are completely red birds (male cardinals) and completely black birds (crows), but most birds are a combination of colors. Remember to look at the pattern of dark and light areas on a bird, as well as its colors. Can you see streaks on the chest, spots on the wings, or a white tail? Noticing these patterns can help you tell similar birds apart.

HOW BIG IS THE BIRD?

It helps to compare a new bird to a common one you already know. For instance, is it bigger than a robin or smaller than a robin? Try thinking of it this way:

- **Tiny**—Hummingbirds
- **Small**—Sparrows, chickadees, wrens
- **Medium**—Robins, jays, blackbirds
- **Large**—Crows, hawks, ducks
- **Huge**—Eagles, herons, pelicans, swans

WHAT SHAPE IS THE BIRD?

Is it tall and slender with long legs for wading in the water? Does it have a crest like a Blue Jay or Northern Cardinal? Or is it small with short legs for hopping on the ground? What is the shape of its bill? You might not be able to give your mystery bird a name just by looking at its shape, but you can often figure out what type of bird it is. For instance, that tall bird with long legs might be a heron and that small bird with short legs hopping on the ground is probably a sparrow.

Western Meadowlark

Bushtit

WHAT IS THE BIRD DOING?

How a bird is behaving or what it is doing can be good clues. If you see a medium-size, black-and-white bird clinging to a tree trunk, it's probably a woodpecker. A large bird soaring high in the sky is probably a hawk or vulture.

USE YOUR EARS

Songs and call notes can be as important as visual clues. Each bird species has its own special songs and calls. Some birds have such memorable songs that they are named for them. Chickadees really do go *chick-a-dee-dee-dee* and the Eastern Phoebe calls out *fee-bee.* Some experienced birders can identify birds just by their songs and calls. Even if you don't recognize a bird's song, it's a great clue to where it may be hiding.

BINOCULARS AND OTHER GEAR

BINOCULARS

It is possible to look at birds without binoculars—for example, at a window feeder or a park where the birds have become tame. But, almost always, binoculars help you see birds much more clearly. Through binoculars the birds will appear close up, so you can see details. And with binoculars, you can easily see birds that are flying high in the sky or feeding up in the treetops.

Many families have a pair of binoculars that are used at sporting events or concerts.

While these may not be ideal binoculars for looking at birds, they are better than no binoculars at all. Ask if you can borrow them and how to adjust them to your eyes, and promise to take good care of them.

HOW TO USE BINOCULARS

First, find a bird with your naked eyes. Then, *without taking your eyes off the bird,* lift the binoculars to your eyes. Usually you'll see the bird right away. Tip: It's almost impossible to find a bird by scanning the trees while looking through the binoculars. And remember to always keep the binoculars strap around your neck.

KEEPING TRACK

A small notebook and a pencil are useful, but not essential. Jot down the date and place and what birds you saw, and any details about the bird that interest you. Later, if you start a life list (a list of all the species you have ever seen), you will have a record of the birds you have already seen. For starters, try keeping a list of the birds you see in your backyard taped to the refrigerator and update it with new birds as you see them.

FIELD GUIDE BOOKS

You can bring along this book when you go bird-watching, but it would be better to concentrate on watching the birds when you're outside and look the birds up in the book later on. There are 100 birds described in this book, but you will also see birds that aren't in this book. As you get more involved in watching birds, you may want to get a field guide with more species in it, like *The National Geographic Backyard Guide to Birds*, or the granddaddy of all field guides: *The National Geographic Field Guide to Birds of North America*.

CLOTHING

Clothing in bright colors, bold patterns, or white can scare birds. If possible, wear tan, dark green or olive, dark blue or brown. Avoid noisy nylon jackets or pants that make loud, swishy noises when you walk. Wearing a baseball-style hat will shield your eyes from the sun's glare and make it easier to see birds in the treetops or soaring high in a sunny sky. Don't wear sunglasses though; they make it impossible to see birds hiding in darker places.

PLAY BY THE RULES

• **Be quiet and careful.** If you make noise, talk in a loud voice, or get too close, the birds will get scared and fly away. Be stealthy and sneak up on birds, so they stay put and you can look at them. You can get fairly close if you try!

• **Don't disturb nesting birds, their nests, eggs, or baby birds.** If you come upon a baby bird on the ground that is not yet able to fly, leave it where it is. Chances are, the baby bird's mother knows where it is and will come to feed it. If it has left the nest, it may be close to being able to fly. Although a baby bird that has left the nest too soon may not make it, baby birds that are "rescued" by people often die. If you're in doubt, call your local Audubon Society or a veterinarian.

• **Respect private and public property.** Ask permission before going onto private property—like yards, country clubs, or private beaches—to look at birds. While in parks or nature preserves, stay on paths, trails, or boardwalks, and don't do anything to damage the environment. When there are no trashcans around, put your litter in your pocket or backpack and take it home with you.

• **HAVE FUN!**

Northern Cardinal

Red-tailed Hawk

AMERICAN ROBIN

Eastern
Backyard
Birds

Eastern Backyard

HABITAT

AMERICAN ROBIN

BLACK-CAPPED CHICKADEE

NORTHERN CARDINAL

ALWAYS SOMETHING NEW!

Birds love the variety of trees and bushes found in eastern backyards, which provide lots of places to nest, gather food, and hide from predators. By adding a bird feeder and a bird-bath to your yard, many species will become year-round residents. Some species will make your backyard their home just during the summer, others will pass through twice a year on migration, and a few will be there only in winter. That's what keeps backyard birding fun—something new is always happening!

MOURNING DOVE

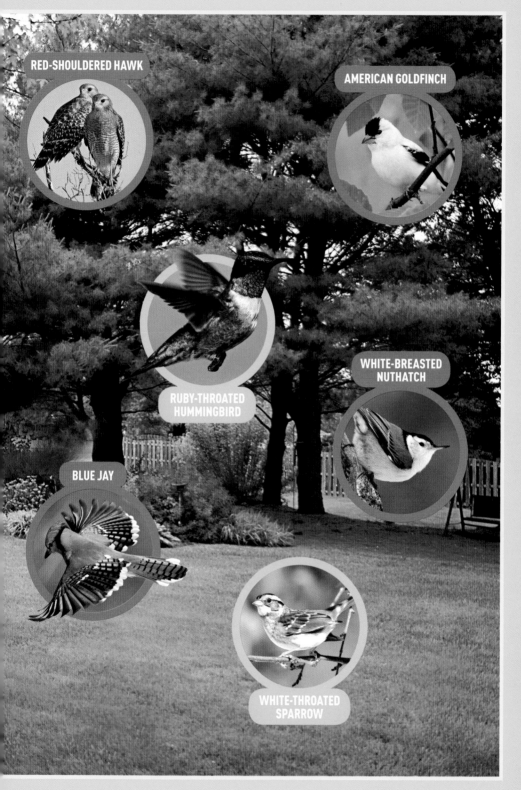

RED-SHOULDERED HAWK

AMERICAN GOLDFINCH

RUBY-THROATED
HUMMINGBIRD

WHITE-BREASTED
NUTHATCH

BLUE JAY

WHITE-THROATED
SPARROW

Ruby-Throated Hummingbird

RUBY-THROATED Hummingbirds are the only species of hummingbird living on the East Coast. These tiny birds can sometimes be seen in groups around a hummingbird feeder or in a flower garden. Ruby-throats are tough and feisty. They chase each other and try to keep other hummingbirds from getting any food. Hummingbirds can beat their wings in a figure-eight motion at 75 times a second, which allows them to hover in one place and even fly sideways and backwards. They burn so much energy that they need to eat all the time and can consume their body weight in food every day. When these birds are flying, their hearts beat an amazing 1,250 times per minute, compared to an active person's 100 to 120.

SCIENTIFIC NAME: *Archilochus colubris*
LENGTH: 3¾ in (10 cm)
WINGSPAN: 4½ in (11 cm)

VITAL STATISTICS

VOICE

Hummingbirds aren't great singers, but they produce soft *tchew* notes and a surprisingly loud series of rapid squeals—*ch'ch'ch' ch'ch*—when chasing away a rival. When a hummingbird is nearby, you can hear a humming sound—like a buzzing bee—made by its rapidly beating wings.

FOOD

A hummingbird laps up nectar—its long tongue has a brushy tip that holds the sugary liquid and pulls it back into its mouth. These birds also eat tiny insects, which are the main food fed to baby hummingbirds. If you put up a hummingbird feeder, you'll get a really close look at these beautiful birds.

HABITAT & RANGE

Ruby-throats spend the spring and summer in parks, gardens, meadows, and along woodland edges across the eastern U.S. and Canada. In winter most fly to Mexico or Central America. The trip from the Texas coast to the Yucatán Peninsula in Mexico is about 500 miles, an amazing, nonstop journey for a bird that weighs less than a penny. Stored body fat is the fuel that powers its flight.

A FEMALE Ruby-throated Hummingbird has a **white** throat and a glittering **green** back.

A CLOSER LOOK

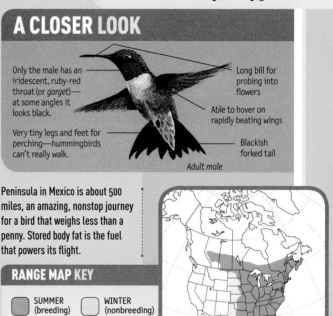

Only the male has an iridescent, ruby-red throat (or *gorget*)—at some angles it looks black.

Very tiny legs and feet for perching—hummingbirds can't really walk.

Long bill for probing into flowers

Able to hover on rapidly beating wings

Blackish forked tail

Adult male

RANGE MAP KEY

SUMMER (breeding)	WINTER (nonbreeding)
MIGRATION	YEAR-ROUND

A THIMBLE-SIZE HOME

Made of dandelion down, tiny wisps of root and grass, and held together with strands of sticky spider's web, the tiny nest of a Ruby-throat is built by the female bird on top of a tree branch—construction takes about five days. She first makes a firm base and then builds up the one-inch walls, forming them between her neck and chest. The walls remain pliable and can stretch as the baby hummingbirds grow. As a final touch, the outside is decorated with flakes of lichen, which may help hide the nest from predators.

Blue Jay

LOUD, COLORFUL, BOSSY, intelligent, thieving, and bold are words that describe Blue Jays. But sometimes—while they are nesting in the summer—Blue Jays are shy and stay hidden. In fall, many jays migrate south in noisy bands, a pretty sight to see as they fly above the changing autumn leaves.

SCIENTIFIC NAME: *Cyanocitta cristata*
LENGTH: 11 in (28 cm)
WINGSPAN: 16 in (41 cm)

If you know where an oak tree grows, that is a great spot to look for a Blue Jay, who has a huge appetite for acorns. In fact, when there are too many acorns to eat, Blue Jays hide them throughout the forest, tucking them under leaves and into brush piles. Sometimes, they forget to retrieve an acorn, and it sprouts—a new oak tree begins life and will someday produce acorns to feed future generations of Blue Jays.

VOICE

All kinds of sounds come out of a Blue Jay's mouth, depending on what it's doing or how it's feeling. When making a fuss, it calls out a piercing *jay, jay, jay!* Quieter sounds include a soft *wheedle-wheedle* and a whistled *tooli.* It often mimics the loud screaming call of the Red-shouldered Hawk (see p. 28), so don't get fooled.

DURING CONFRONTATIONS Blue Jays try to look as **large** as possible.

FOOD

Blue Jays—like people—are omnivores, that is, they eat lots of different foods: nuts, seeds, fruits, insects, worms, and even other birds' eggs and small animals like frogs or mice. Sometimes they search for food in the treetops, and sometimes they look on the ground. Blue Jays are more than happy to eat cracked corn, peanuts, or suet at a bird feeder, where they often chase smaller birds away until they have had their fill.

A CLOSER LOOK

A large throat pouch (hidden) can expand to carry two or three acorns.

White spots on blue wings

Long tail feathers with white tips

Crest, sometimes flattened

Blackish necklace

HABITAT & RANGE

If you live just about anywhere in the East, chances are you've seen this bird. It likes forests, especially oak forests, but is also quite content to live in a tree-filled city park or suburban backyard. Birds living in far northern areas migrate south in the fall, but, in most areas of the East, Blue Jays can be seen year-round.

RANGE MAP KEY

SUMMER (breeding)

WINTER (nonbreeding)

YEAR-ROUND

CHECK OUT MY CREST

Just as a frown or smile lets you know how a friend is feeling, the Blue Jay's crest signals to nearby birds if it is relaxed or mad. When the bird is sitting on its nest, feeding its nestlings, or just hanging out with its mate or family, its crest is flattened. When it is feeling threatened or aggressive, its crest is held up. The higher the crest, the more agitated the Blue Jay.

23

American Robin

WHEN THE EARLY COLONISTS arrived in North America they saw a bird that reminded them of a common bird from back home in Europe, so they gave it the same name: Robin. The name stuck, even though our American Robin is a member of the thrush family and isn't related to the European Robin. The American Robin, common all across the U.S., is easy to recognize with its reddish breast, upright stance, and potbellied look. Watch a robin make its way across a grassy lawn in search of something squirmy to eat. It moves in a jerky run-stop-run pattern, then stops and cocks its head to look for an earthworm or grub. After a long winter, a sure sign that spring has arrived is the male robin singing his loud song.

SCIENTIFIC NAME: *Turdus migratorius*
LENGTH: 10 in (25 cm)
WINGSPAN: 17 in (43 cm)

VOICE

The male robin's loud and lively song has a bubbly quality. It's made up of short phrases: *cheerily-cheer up-cheerio.* Males and females both give soft clucking calls and a variety of shrill alarm calls.

FOOD

Robins eat earthworms, but that's not all. Robins also poke around under fallen leaves in search of insects. During the winter, most robins switch to a diet of fruits and berries. You can often see groups of robins feeding in holly trees and other plants with red berries. After the berries are gone, the flock moves on to a different location.

HABITAT & RANGE

Robins are widespread and common, so you should be able to see them wherever you live in North America. They are found in a variety of wooded areas, open fields, and urban and suburban areas. In summer, they nest as far north as Alaska, almost to the Arctic Ocean. Most robins migrate in a southern direction, sometimes

A YOUNG ROBIN has a heavily **spotted** breast.

A CLOSER LOOK

White crescents around the eye

Brick red underparts

Yellow bill

Strong legs are good for walking and running.

in large flocks, so the birds that you see in winter may be different from the ones that nested in your backyard in summer.

RANGE MAP KEY

- SUMMER (breeding)
- WINTER (nonbreeding)
- YEAR-ROUND

HOME SWEET HOME

Some sturdy sticks, a little dried grass, all glued together with some sticky mud—it's a bit untidy, but a robin's nest is just temporary housing. After construction, the female lays four blue eggs and sits on them (incubates them) for 12 to 14 days until they hatch. The baby robins grow quickly and leave the nest after about two weeks, never to return. Robins aren't shy around people, and sometimes they even nest under a porch roof or on a protected windowsill.

Northern Cardinal

THE BRIGHT RED male Northern Cardinal ("redbird") might be America's most popular bird. Because of its colorful plumage and stylish good looks, the cardinal is the official state bird of seven states—Illinois, Indiana, Kentucky, North Carolina, Ohio, Virginia, and West Virginia—more than any other species. People often think that every bright red bird they see is a cardinal, even though some tanagers and finches are equally red. If you want to know for sure, look for the cardinal's crest and massive red bill. Cardinals used to be seen mostly in the American South, but they have expanded their range far to the north and west since the 19th century because of changes in habitat and warming temperatures.

SCIENTIFIC NAME: *Cardinalis cardinalis*
LENGTH: 8¾ in (22 cm)
WINGSPAN: 12 in (30 cm)

VOICE

Unlike many other birds, male and female cardinals both sing, sometimes in a duet. They have a variety of songs, but a loud whistled *what-cheer! what-cheer! what-cheer!* or *purty-purty-purty* are common. Their call note is a sharp *pik*.

FOOD

Cardinals eat different foods at different times of the year. In spring and summer, their food is mostly insects with some flower buds, berries, and weed seeds mixed in. In winter their favorite foods are seeds and some berries. A bird feeder stocked with black-oil sunflower seeds is sure to attract any cardinals living in your neighborhood.

HABITAT & RANGE

Cardinals are widespread and common in the East and Midwest, and abundant in the southern U.S. They like brushy habitats like woodland edges, thickets, vine tangles, shrubby backyards, and city parks. Surprisingly, Northern

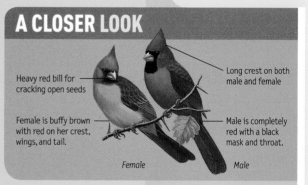

A BABY Northern Cardinal may **leave** its nest before being able to fly. Its **parents** will follow it around and feed it.

A CLOSER LOOK

Heavy red bill for cracking open seeds

Long crest on both male and female

Female is buffy brown with red on her crest, wings, and tail.

Male is completely red with a black mask and throat.

Female　　　*Male*

Cardinals also live in the desert Southwest in dense shrubs and along riverbeds. These birds do not migrate. Instead they live in the same place all year long.

RANGE MAP KEY

YEAR-ROUND

WHAT THE HECK!

In the spring the feisty male Northern Cardinal, like most birds, establishes his nesting territory and defends it from others of his own species. Unfortunately, evolution has not taught him about reflections. A male cardinal will attack his own reflection in a car mirror thinking it is another bird moving in on his space.

Mini-Profiles

EASTERN BACKYARD

Here are a few more of the many birds that live in eastern backyards. All of these birds—except the hawk—love to eat seeds from a bird feeder or scattered on the ground.

RED-SHOULDERED HAWK

SCIENTIFIC NAME: *Buteo lineatus*
LENGTH: 17 in (43 cm)
WINGSPAN: 40 in (102 cm)

The colorful Red-shouldered Hawk is a very vocal bird with a loud screaming call, *KEE-ahh*. When you hear its call, look up to see it soaring over wooded backyards. To catch its prey, the hawk perches quietly at the edge of the woods and then pounces down on small mammals and reptiles.

MOURNING DOVE

SCIENTIFIC NAME: *Zenaida macroura*
LENGTH: 12 in (31 cm)
WINGSPAN: 18 in (46 cm)

There are the same number of Mourning Doves living in the U.S. as there are people—about 350 million. They live in open areas including suburban yards. Listen for the dove's slow, mournful call, *oowoo-woo-woo-woo*, and the whistling sound made by its wings when it bursts into flight. You can attract doves to your backyard by scattering birdseed on the ground.

BLACK-CAPPED CHICKADEE

SCIENTIFIC NAME: *Poecile atricapillus*
LENGTH: 5¼ in (13 cm)
WINGSPAN: 8 in (20 cm)

Chickadees are cute little birds that aren't very afraid of people and that love to come to bird feeders. The Black-capped and Carolina Chickadees are almost identical (black cap and throat, white cheek, and gray back), but the Black-capped lives in northern areas, while the Carolina lives in the southern U.S. The chickadee is named for its call: *chick-a-dee-dee-dee.*

WHITE-BREASTED NUTHATCH

SCIENTIFIC NAME: *Sitta carolinensis*
LENGTH: 5¾ in (15 cm)
WINGSPAN: 11 in (28 cm)

If you see a small gray-and-white bird climbing nimbly up, down, and around a tree trunk, chances are good that you've spotted a White-breasted Nuthatch. The nuthatch has an extra-long hind claw that helps it get a grip in any position. It lives year-round in woods and wooded backyards and is crazy about suet feeders. Its call is a low-pitched nasal *yank*.

WHITE-THROATED SPARROW

SCIENTIFIC NAME: *Zonotrichia albicollis*
LENGTH: 6¾ in (17 cm)
WINGSPAN: 9 in (23 cm)

In the spring, these sparrows travel to northern areas to breed, but in the winter they are very common around backyards and forest edges. Feed them by scattering seed on the ground and you might get a large flock hanging around all winter. Take a close look and you'll see that some sparrows have black-and-white head stripes (the hard-core aggressive birds) and others have tan-and-white stripes (the laid-back passive birds). This has nothing to do with being male or female, and successful breeding pairs usually consist of one of each type. Its song sounds like "Old Sam Peabody, Peabody, Peabody."

AMERICAN GOLDFINCH

SCIENTIFIC NAME: *Spinus tristis*
LENGTH: 5 in (13 cm)
WINGSPAN: 9 in (23 cm)

From spring to fall, male goldfinches have dazzling yellow plumage and a black cap and wings. In the winter, males are a more subdued tan color, as are the females year-round. Goldfinches are common in overgrown fields, backyards, and along roadsides across the continent, and they like to visit bird feeders. The goldfinch is the state bird of Iowa, New Jersey, and Washington. Its flight call *per-chik-o-ree* sounds like "po-ta-to chip."

ANNA'S HUMMINGBIRD

Western
Backyard
Birds

Western Backyard
HABITAT

ANNA'S HUMMINGBIRD

ACORN WOODPECKER

A TREASURE TROVE OF BIRDS!

The western states of California, Oregon, and Washington, and the Canadian province of British Columbia are chock-full of amazing birds. In this chapter you'll get to know ten bird species that live all over the West and show up in backyards. Whether you live in San Diego, California, or Seattle, Washington, you have a good chance of seeing all or most of them. Keep your eyes open and you'll see lots of other birds too, especially if you can put up a bird feeder.

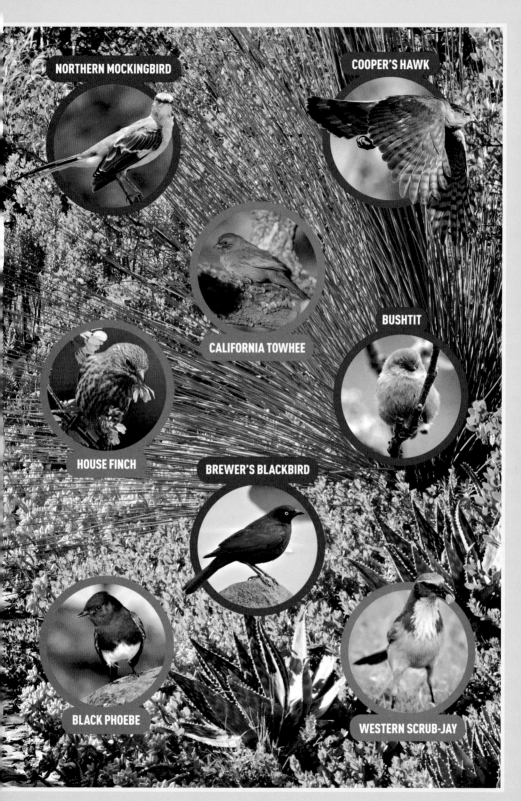

NORTHERN MOCKINGBIRD

COOPER'S HAWK

CALIFORNIA TOWHEE

BUSHTIT

HOUSE FINCH

BREWER'S BLACKBIRD

BLACK PHOEBE

WESTERN SCRUB-JAY

33

Anna's Hummingbird

ANNA'S HUMMINGBIRDS are the most common hummingbirds along the Pacific coast. Backyard gardens with lots of flowers and a hummingbird feeder are a magnet for them. Most male hummingbirds have a shining jewel-like throat, but the male Anna's has even more bling—the top of his head glows rose red like his throat. When the sun hits it just right, it's like a magical ruby spotlight was turned on. Then, with a shift of his head, the light goes off and the feathers look black. (The way the color and light is created is called iridescence.) Native Americans revered hummingbirds and had many legends about them. One story describes how the hummingbird used its sharp, pointed bill to poke holes in the black sky and created stars.

SCIENTIFIC NAME: *Calypte anna*
LENGTH: 4 in (10 cm)
WINGSPAN: 5¼ in (13 cm)

VOICE

The male Anna's Hummingbird carries a pretty good tune, but to human ears it sounds more like a jumble of high-pitched squeaks and scratchy notes. The male and female give high, sharp calls *chit, chit, chid-it, chit.* When they are chasing away rival hummingbirds, listen for a rapid series of rattle-like calls *jika, jika, jika.*

FOOD

Like the Ruby-throat (see pp. 20–21), these humming-birds use their long tongue to lap up nectar from flowers. They also eat tiny insects, which are the main food fed to baby hummingbirds. You might see a hummingbird poking into shallow holes in a tree trunk that were made by a woodpecker—it's feeding on the sugary tree sap and any insects attracted to it.

HABITAT & RANGE

One hundred years ago Anna's Hummingbirds lived only in southern California and northern Baja California (in Mexico). Today their range extends north to Canada. What changed? People planted gardens of

> **FEMALES** build nests and care for **babies** without help from males.

A CLOSER LOOK

Only the male has an iridescent red throat and crown—at some angles it looks black (females have a few red feathers on their throats).

Adult male

Young males have patchy red throats.

Zooms around backyards on buzzing wings.

exotic flowering plants and trees, and the hummingbirds followed. In the warm climate, the birds can find flower nectar even in winter, so they don't migrate.

RANGE MAP KEY

SUMMER (breeding)	WINTER (nonbreeding)
YEAR-ROUND	

CHOOSE ME!

To impress a female Anna's Hummingbird, the male has an awesome display flight. You might even see one in your backyard. It starts with the male hummingbird hovering in front of the female, and then flying straight up to over 100 feet. From there he plummets in a high-speed dive to within inches of the perched female, making a loud *PEEK!* sound with his tail feathers as he pulls out of the dive. The performance finishes with a "shuttle display" as he flies back and forth a foot above the female, while singing his squeaky love song. Sometimes a charged-up male will even display to a nearby person.

Acorn Woodpecker

ACORN WOODPECKERS are great fun to watch. They love company, living in colonies of a dozen or more related birds that might include aunts, uncles, brothers, sisters, and, of course, mom and dad. They all work together to gather and store thousands of acorns in a special storage tree (granary tree) so that the colony will have food in the winter months. The granary tree is the center of the colony and it's not unusual for groups of birds to gather there, calling loudly and flashing their wings in a woodpecker greeting. The birds also share other chores and responsibilities. One-year-old birds don't breed, but they stay with the colony and help raise the baby birds by feeding and caring for them.

SCIENTIFIC NAME: *Melanerpes formicivorus*
LENGTH: 9¼ in (24 cm)
WINGSPAN: 17½ in (44 cm)

VITAL STATISTICS

VOICE

Very noisy! Acorn Woodpeckers don't sing, but they loudly call *wakka-wakka-wakka* or *ja-cob, ja-cob, ja-cob.* Sometimes groups gather on a tree limb and call back and forth while spreading their flashy wings. The zany calls of the Acorn Woodpecker inspired Walter Lantz to create the famous cartoon character Woody Woodpecker.

FOOD

Obviously, Acorn Woodpeckers have a taste for acorns, but they eat other things as well. On warm days they catch flying insects by spying them from a high perch and snatching them in flight (flycatching). Wild fruit and tree sap are also on their diet.

HABITAT & RANGE

Look for these western birds wherever oak trees occur, in mountain forests, backyards, and even city parks. If they're around, these noisy birds are hard to miss. A colony of Acorn Woodpeckers

> IN FLIGHT or when calling, the Acorn Woodpecker flashes the **white** feathers in its wings and on its rump.

A CLOSER LOOK

Female

Clownlike face pattern and white eyes

Male

Glossy black back with white patches in the wings and on the rump

Stiff, black tail feathers, used for support when clinging to a tree trunk

defends its feeding territory—usually a grove of oak trees—and lives in the same place year-round. The only reason they might wander is if they can't find food.

RANGE MAP KEY

☐ YEAR-ROUND

ONE FOR ALL AND ALL FOR ONE

The members of an Acorn Woodpecker colony spend lots of time storing acorns by drilling holes that exactly fit the acorns. A single tree (known as a granary tree) may have thousands and thousands of stored acorns for all the birds in the colony to share. Backyard Acorn Woodpeckers sometimes choose a telephone pole or even the side of a wooden house to drill into. If a squirrel, jay, or woodpecker from a different colony tries to steal acorns from them, the whole colony drives the thief away with lots of loud calls and swooping attacks.

Western Scrub-Jay

WESTERN SCRUB-JAYS ARE very smart birds, like their relatives the crows and ravens. They always seem to be figuring out an angle that will score them an easy meal or some kind of advantage. They're not above stealing food from other birds that they can intimidate or outwit. Sometimes a jay will spy on another jay that has some food it is trying to hide. Afterward, it sneaks in and takes the food from the other bird's hiding place. When they are stashing food away, most jays learn to look around first and make sure that they aren't being spied on. When a predator, such as a snake or owl, is spotted, a jay will shriek for minutes at a time, warning others about the danger.

SCIENTIFIC NAME: *Aphelocoma californica*
LENGTH: 11 in (28 cm)
WINGSPAN: 15½ in (39 cm)

VOICE

Although not a musical singer, the Western Scrub-Jay's calls are very loud and attract a lot of attention. The most common call is a harsh, up-slurred *jaaay?* or *jreeee?* that sounds like a question being asked. When jays are in flight or upset about something, you might hear a noisy series of *shee-yuk, shee-yuk, shee-yuk* calls.

SCRUB-JAYS often **chase** smaller birds away from a feeder.

FOOD

Like the Blue Jay that lives in the East, the Western Scrub-Jay eats a variety of foods, usually whatever is easiest to find or capture. Sometimes the meal is vegetarian (seeds, nuts, fruit) and other times it's animal (insects, small lizards, bird's eggs). Scrub-Jays are also frequent visitors to bird feeders, where they especially like peanuts and sunflower seeds.

A CLOSER LOOK

Azure blue head with a white eyebrow

Rounded head, similar to the Steller's Jay, which also lives in the West, but has a tall crest

Heavy, black bill is an all-purpose tool.

Mostly blue above with a blue breast band

Short wings and long tail make it easy to fly in tight places.

HABITAT & RANGE

Western Scrub-Jays are found in many different places. In the wild, they live in oak woodlands or brushy areas, but they are very adaptable and are quite happy to live in a backyard or a city park. They don't migrate. A pair—male and female—stays together throughout the year. During the nesting season they will chase off other jays that might try to move into their home territory. In the winter they're friendlier to each other and sometimes hang out together in flocks.

RANGE MAP KEY

☐ WINTER (nonbreeding)   ◼ YEAR-ROUND

HIDE AND SEEK

Did you ever hide something and then forget where you put it? That hardly ever happens to a Western Scrub-Jay. When acorns or pine nuts are abundant, a jay will hide hundreds of them—under a rock, in a bark crevice, behind some twigs, almost anywhere. Amazingly, the jay—unlike a human—will remember where almost all of them are stashed, even months later. Scientists aren't sure how the birds do it.

Northern Mockingbird

HAVE YOU EVER HEARD a bird singing late at night? If you answer yes, you probably have a Northern Mockingbird living in your neighborhood. A male mockingbird sometimes sings all night long, trying to attract attention from a female. This songbird is truly an awe-inspiring singer, "sampling" the songs of many other birds into his own creation. He will repeat each song snippet three or more times and then move on to a different one. A single mockingbird can sing hundreds of different song fragments. Females sing too, although they do it more quietly and less often. Mockingbirds (and all wild birds) are protected, so it's against the law to keep them as pets, but you can enjoy them singing in your backyard.

SCIENTIFIC NAME: *Mimus polyglottos*
LENGTH: 10 in (25 cm)
WINGSPAN: 14 in (36 cm)

VOICE

Males and females both sing. The mockingbird adds the songs of many other birds into his performance (mimicry). Most of the long-winded song is composed of pleasant whistles, but the mockingbird adds in harsh scolds and trills. When chasing a rival away from a thicket full of berries, an angry mockingbird calls out a high raspy *skeeh, skeeh, skeeh.*

FOOD

The mockingbird eats a full menu of insects in spring and summer. Winter food is mostly berries, and many mockingbirds claim a favorite berry patch and chase off all other birds that get too close.

HABITAT & RANGE

Northern Mockingbirds are common from east to west, but they avoid colder areas like Canada and the northern states. They prefer to live in hedges and thickets with nearby open areas or lawns. Big backyards and overgrown fields are perfect, but they also live around

YOUNG mockingbirds look different than their parents; they have dark eyes and **spotted** breasts.

A CLOSER LOOK

Adults have yellow eyes.

Males and females look the same.

White patches in the dark wings and tail (best seen in flight)

Gray and white feathers

Adult

Juvenile

suburban housing tracts and city parks with ornamental trees and shrubs. Most mockingbirds live in the same place all year long.

RANGE MAP KEY

SUMMER (breeding)

WINTER (nonbreeding)

YEAR-ROUND

A FLASH OF WHITE

When a Northern Mockingbird is on the ground searching for a meal in the grass, you might see it stop suddenly and flash its wings open in a series of jerks—showing off its big white wing patches. Scientists aren't sure why the mockingbird does this so often; maybe it startles any insects hiding in the grass and makes it easier to catch them. Or, it might be a signal to other mockingbirds to stay away.

Many birds don't need wilderness places to live in—they do just fine with people for neighbors. Here are six more western backyard birds that you can look for.

COOPER'S HAWK

SCIENTIFIC NAME: *Accipiter cooperii*
LENGTH: 17 in (43 cm)
WINGSPAN: 32 in (81 cm)

The Cooper's Hawk survives by hunting and eating smaller birds. Backyards with bird feeders are often visited by a Cooper's Hawk looking to ambush a distracted bird. In the air, its long tail works like a rudder, so it can turn on a dime. And its supersharp talons easily grab a flying bird. If a particular hawk bothers your bird feeder too often, take the feeder down for a few days until the hawk moves on.

BLACK PHOEBE

SCIENTIFIC NAME: *Sayornis nigricans*
LENGTH: 6¾ in (17 cm)
WINGSPAN: 11 in (28 cm)

The only black-and-white flycatcher in North America, the Black Phoebe is elegantly dressed in what resembles a black shirt and white pants. Active and trusting, this little bird darts out to catch flying insects and scarcely notices people nearby. Black Phoebes are often seen in places where there is water, like a wild stream or lake, as well as around backyard swimming pools and park fountains.

BUSHTIT

SCIENTIFIC NAME: *Psaltriparus minimus*
LENGTH: 4½ in (13 cm)
WINGSPAN: 8 in (20 cm)

Yes, Bushtit really is its common name! You hardly ever see just one Bushtit; they live in small flocks of 10 to 40 birds that stay close together all year. They are tiny, mostly gray birds with a ball-shaped body and a long tail, and are a common resident of backyard gardens and parks as well as wilder places. The Bushtit's nest is a remarkable hanging home that is woven of plant fibers and spider webs and then decorated with bits of other plants to keep it hidden (camouflaged). It may take more than a month to build.

CALIFORNIA TOWHEE

SCIENTIFIC NAME: *Pipilo crissalis*
LENGTH: 9 in (23 cm)
WINGSPAN: 11½ in (29 cm)

The California Towhee is sort of drab-looking—mostly brown with a little rusty orange color under its tail—and it rarely moves far from where it nests. It's a type of large sparrow, and if you live in California there's a good chance there's a pair living in your neighborhood. Pairs stay together all year and often call back and forth *chink, chink, chink* to each other as they scratch at the ground hunting for seeds or insects hidden under fallen leaves. They also like to eat birdseed and cracked corn scattered on the ground.

BREWER'S BLACKBIRD

SCIENTIFIC NAME: *Euphagus cyanocephalus*
LENGTH: 9 in (23 cm)
WINGSPAN: 15 in (38 cm)

Brewer's Blackbirds are survivors and have actually become more common across most of North America in places where people live and farm. They do well in backyards and along city streets, where you might find a small flock looking for fallen food scraps under the tables of an outdoor restaurant. Although they look simply black most of the time, when the full sun reflects off the male's glossy plumage you'll see the most beautiful combination of metallic green, rich purple, and deep blue.

HOUSE FINCH

SCIENTIFIC NAME: *Carpodacus mexicanus*
LENGTH: 6 in (15 cm)
WINGSPAN: 9½ in (24 cm)

At one time, House Finches lived only in the West. After some caged House Finches were released on Long Island in 1940, they eventually spread throughout the East and are now very common all across the United States. They eat seeds and have a thick bill for cracking them open. The male has a bright red head and breast. The female has streaky brown plumage that is good camouflage when she is sitting on her nest, which she sometimes builds under a porch or in a hanging planter.

City
Streets and Parks

HOUSE SPARROW

City Streets and Parks

HABITAT

MONK PARAKEET

HOUSE SPARROW

EUROPEAN STARLING

STREET LIFE

CHIMNEY SWIFT

City streets might not look like a place where any birds would want to live. How does a bird find a meal or raise a nestful of baby birds in a big city? In fact, for some birds the city is an ideal place. There is a population boom among the bird species that can meet the challenges of street life in our cities. If you live in a city near a park with trees and a pond, you'll see even more species.

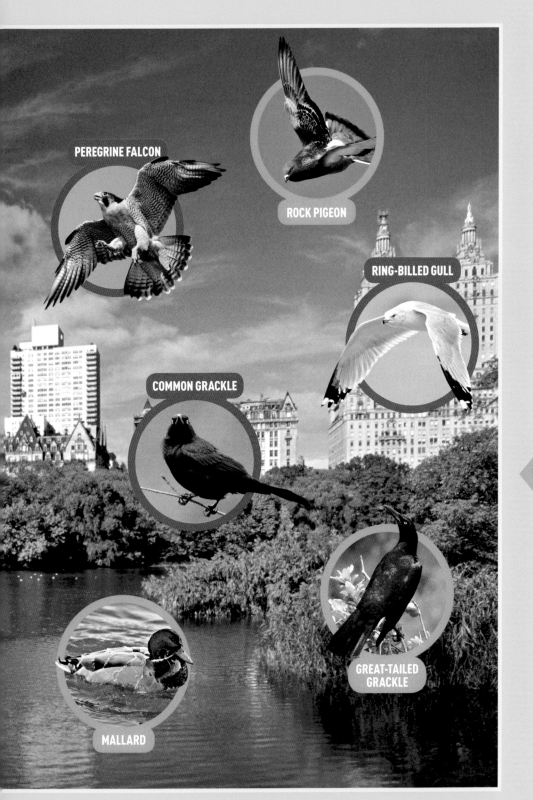

PEREGRINE FALCON

ROCK PIGEON

RING-BILLED GULL

COMMON GRACKLE

GREAT-TAILED GRACKLE

MALLARD

Peregrine Falcon

THE PEREGRINE FALCON WOULD be an Olympic gold medalist in the bird world. It holds the world record for speed among birds—over 200 miles an hour. This speedy bird eats other birds. It attacks its prey by dropping down from high above in a spectacular high-speed dive called a stoop. With its large, powerful feet, the Peregrine hits its prey, stunning or killing it, and then grabs it before it hits the ground. In the wild, Peregrines breed where there are cliffs for nesting, but in recent years many have taken up the city life. Ledges on tall skyscrapers, water towers, and bridges take the place of cliffs, and there are plenty of city pigeons to feed on.

SCIENTIFIC NAME: *Falco peregrinus*
LENGTH: 17 in (43 cm)
WINGSPAN: 41 in (104 cm)

VOICE

Falcons are usually silent. Around their nest they give a rapid series of harsh calls—*kak-kak-kak*—when upset or communicating with their young.

FOOD

Peregrine Falcons eat mostly birds, caught and killed in flight and then taken to a perch to be plucked and eaten. In North America, over 450 different species have been documented as prey, from tiny hummingbirds to giant Sandhill Cranes, but most are medium-size birds like ducks, sandpipers, and pigeons. Peregrines also hunt bats if they are available and sometimes steal the prey of other raptors.

HABITAT & RANGE

Peregrine Falcons were almost extinct in eastern North America about 50 years ago because of a pesticide called DDT that got into their bodies. When DDT was banned in 1972, the falcons started to recover and now are no longer endangered. Peregrine Falcons live in many places from coastal cities to high mountains and occur on every continent except Antarctica. The name

YOUNG PEREGRINES (juveniles) are **browner** than their parents and are streaked underneath. This one lives on the side of a **skyscraper.**

A CLOSER LOOK

Juvenile

Blue-gray above with a blackish hood

Black wedge of feathers below the eye helps reduce the sun's glare, just like the black face paint used by some football and baseball players.

Adult

Large feet with sharp talons to grasp prey

Hooked bill for plucking feathers and tearing flesh

Pointed wings are built for speed.

Long tail makes quick, high-speed turns possible.

"peregrine" means wanderer, and some Peregrine Falcons that nest in the Arctic wander as far as South America during the winter months.

RANGE MAP KEY

SUMMER (breeding)

WINTER (nonbreeding)

MIGRATION

YEAR-ROUND

FALCONRY—THE SPORT OF KINGS

People have trained falcons for hunting for over 2,000 years. Many different types of hawks and falcons have been used, but the Peregrine and its larger relative the Gyrfalcon have always been the most prized. In early times these birds were reserved for the use of royalty. Today most falcons used for hunting were hatched in captivity, and owning one requires a special permit. Training a young falcon to hunt and come back to its owner takes months of dedicated work. At some airports, trained falcons are used to scare off flocks of birds that might collide with an airplane.

Rock Pigeon

SCIENTIFIC NAME: *Columba livia*
LENGTH: 12½ in (32 cm)
WINGSPAN: 28 in (71 cm)

DURING THE 1600s, European immigrants brought the Rock Pigeon to America. Over the centuries, pigeons have spread throughout North and South America. Most pigeons live near people, especially in towns and cities, where they often nest on building ledges. The Rock Pigeon is a common sight in cities all around the world. Most pigeons are blue-gray with two dark wing bars. Many variations exist—from pure white to rusty brown to checkered—even in a single flock. The Rock Pigeon is also the ancestor of all domesticated pigeons. Many people around the globe keep pigeons as a hobby—breeding, training, and even racing them. In the same way that there are different dog breeds, there are hundreds of pigeon breeds.

VOICE

Courting birds make a series of throaty cooing sounds, *coo-cuk-cuk-cuk-cooo*. During courtship the male struts around the female while cooing, bowing, and inflating his throat. When taking flight, the pigeon's wings make a loud clapping sound.

FOOD

City birds will gather around anyone handing out bread-crumbs or other food tidbits, often eating right from the hand. In parks and on city streets they peck at the ground in search of seeds and other food. Baby pigeons are fed "pigeon's milk," a milky secretion from the bird's crop (part of its throat, also used for storing food).

HABITAT & RANGE

Rock Pigeons don't migrate; they live in the same place all year, even in the coldest areas. City streets and parks are often full of pigeons; in fact it's hard to avoid them in many cities. They also live in suburban and rural areas, especially around farm buildings. Pigeons found in city streets and parks are usually very tame.

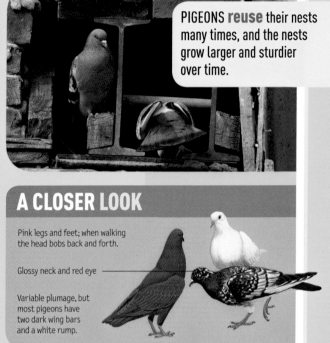

PIGEONS **reuse** their nests many times, and the nests grow larger and sturdier over time.

A CLOSER LOOK

Pink legs and feet; when walking the head bobs back and forth.

Glossy neck and red eye

Variable plumage, but most pigeons have two dark wing bars and a white rump.

RANGE MAP KEY

YEAR-ROUND

WORLD WAR II HERO

The Dickin Medal, awarded to military animals for conspicuous gallantry during wartime, was given to G.I. Joe, a WWII carrier pigeon credited with preventing an Allied-occupied Italian village from being bombed. After receiving the medal in 1946, G.I. Joe served out his retirement at Fort Monmouth, New Jersey, and died in 1961 at the age of 18.

European Starling

EUROPEAN STARLINGS are tough birds to like. They are an invasive species, imported from Europe by immigrants. They're aggressive, pushing native birds like woodpeckers, bluebirds, and titmice out of their nest holes and taking them over. During nesting season they fight with each other over territory. They don't sing nicely, and there are millions of them. On the other hand, when the sun hits their plumage just right it glows with a glossy shine of green and purple, and it's a thrilling sight to see a winter flock take to the sky all at once. In early summer you are likely to see the black-feathered parents followed around by brownish juveniles begging for food, before they learn to find their own meals.

SCIENTIFIC NAME: *Sturnus vulgaris*
LENGTH: 8½ in (22 cm)
WINGSPAN: 16 in (41 cm)

VOICE

The starling's song—if you can call it that—is an amazing mix of rattles, buzzes, clicks, and squealing notes, such as *zzzrt, pssst, pop, wheeeooo, shewheeeer.* They also copy (mimic) the songs of many other birds.

FOOD

Starlings are not picky eaters, which could be the reason there are so many of them. They eat almost anything and are especially fond of insects, spiders, and earthworms, searching for them by digging around in the grass with their pointed bills. They also eat fruits, berries, and seeds.

HABITAT & RANGE

European Starlings prefer to live where people do. During the nesting season the male fights off other birds that want its nest site—usually an old woodpecker hole, a sheltered spot on the side of a building, or a birdhouse meant for another type of bird. In the city they nest in streetlights and traffic signals. In winter they're friendlier

YOUNG starlings have brown feathers, but grow glossy adult **feathers** by the time they are **one** year old.

A CLOSER LOOK

Pointed yellow bill used for prying apart blades of grass in search of insects; bill turns black in winter.

Chunky body

Glossy green and purple plumage, otherwise looks black; in fall and winter its body is covered with white spots.

Short tail and pointed wings

Adult

and hang out in flocks with blackbirds, grackles, and other starlings. Some winter flocks contain thousands of birds. Starlings live in every U.S. state and Canadian province.

RANGE MAP KEY

SUMMER (breeding)

YEAR-ROUND

SHAKESPEARE AND THE STARLING

It's because of the famous writer William Shakespeare that we are overwhelmed with starlings. In 1890, a group of people who loved Shakespeare's work thought it would be a great idea to bring to the United States every bird mentioned in his plays and poetry. Oops, bad idea. They released about 100 starlings in New York City's Central Park and the birds spread fast. By 1950 they could be found from coast to coast. Today about 200 million starlings live in North America.

House Sparrow

HOUSE SPARROWS originally came from Europe and Asia, but they didn't fly here on their own. As with European Starlings (see pp. 52–53), immigrants brought them here. One hundred House Sparrows were released in Brooklyn in 1851. By 1943 their population in North America was 150 million birds. How was that huge increase in numbers possible? First, House Sparrows like to live near people and can survive where most other birds can't. Second, they are very successful at raising families. A single pair usually nests three or four times every year and raises about 20 chicks. In five years a single pair could increase to 1,250 birds. Third, they are tough competitors that can take over nest sites from native birds.

SCIENTIFIC NAME: *Passer domesticus*
LENGTH: 6¼ in (16 cm)
WINGSPAN: 9½ in (24 cm)

VITAL STATISTICS

VOICE

The House Sparrow's most common call is a honest-to-goodness *chirp* or *cheep*. In winter, when birds flock together, their chattering can sound like a room full of talkative people.

FOOD

On city streets it's hard to tell what House Sparrows are finding to eat when they peck at the pavement, even if you watch closely. They are looking for tiny scraps of food that have collected in the cracks. In summer, House Sparrows also seek out grassy areas and shrubs to search for insects. Sometimes they even pick dead insects off car grills. In winter, they survive mostly on weed seeds and food scraps.

HABITAT & RANGE

House Sparrows are very common in most cities. Crevices and ledges on city buildings, suburban houses, and backyards offer places for nesting. In city parks they also nest in old woodpecker holes. The rough-and-tumble male House Sparrow often takes a nest hole away from a less

IN WINTER, House Sparrows form small flocks and **defend** a sheltered place to spend the night.

A CLOSER LOOK

Heavy bill for cracking seeds and catching large insects

Male's black throat and upper chest looks like a bib—the male with the biggest bib is at the top of the pecking order and the first to feed.

Male has black, reddish brown, and gray feathers; female looks brownish with darker streaks.

Fall male

Summer male

Chunky body and big head

Strong legs and feet used for hopping on the ground

aggressive bird, such as a chickadee, titmouse, or bluebird. House Sparrows were also introduced to South America, southern Africa, Australia, and New Zealand.

RANGE MAP KEY

YEAR-ROUND

OPEN SESAME!

Turns out House Sparrows have some amazing ways of getting something to eat. Some birds in Australia figured out that a fast-food restaurant had doors that automatically opened when an "electric eye" was tripped. Male House Sparrows learned to flutter in front of it until the doors opened; then they flew in to pick dinner off the floor. Some females had a different tactic. They perched right on the electric eye and leaned over until the switch was tripped and the door opened. Not bad for a "bird brain."

Mini-Profiles

CITY STREETS AND PARKS

City parks are bird magnets. The park doesn't need to be big, and if it includes a grove of tall trees or a small pond, even better. See if you can spot some of the city and parks birds shown here.

MALLARD

SCIENTIFIC NAME: *Anas platyrhynchos*
LENGTH: 23 in (58 cm)
WINGSPAN: 35 in (89 cm)

The Mallard is the most abundant duck in the world and the ancestor of almost all domestic ducks. Just about every city park with a pond has a flock of half-tame Mallards in a zany mix of colors. Some are migratory wild birds, but others are year-round residents who vary from all-white to all-green to a patchwork of in-between colors. Most food is obtained by "tipping up"—using the familiar "butt-in-the-air-and-head-underwater" position that allows food to be picked off the pond bottom. City ducks are always on the lookout for a handout from visitors.

RING-BILLED GULL

SCIENTIFIC NAME: *Larus delawarensis*
LENGTH: 17½ in (45 cm)
WINGSPAN: 48 in (122 cm)

Many Ring-billed Gulls never go near the ocean, so calling them "seagulls" isn't really correct; "gulls" is a better term. Ring-bills nest in the north, but in winter they are common in and around cities. Flocks of winter gulls can often be seen flying overhead in the morning and evening. They are "commuting" from a safe place to spend the night (perhaps a river island) to a favorite place to feed, and back again. City dumps attract gulls that pick through the garbage for a "recycled" meal.

MONK PARAKEET

SCIENTIFIC NAME: *Myiopsitta monachus*
LENGTH: 11½ in (29 cm)
WINGSPAN: 19 in (48 cm)

Yes, there really are parrots living in cities, and not only in "tropical" Miami or Los Angeles. Monk Parakeets are native to South America, but they are able to withstand the freezing temperatures of cities as far north as Chicago and New York. Many are pet birds that escaped their cages or were set free by their owners to form small colonies in the wild. They build large ball-like nests from thousands of sticks. A single nest can be home to a dozen or more families and is used throughout the year for shelter.

CHIMNEY SWIFT

SCIENTIFIC NAME: *Chaetura pelagica*
LENGTH: 5¼ in (13 cm)
WINGSPAN: 14 in (36 cm)

The Chimney Swift looks like a "cigar with wings." Swifts spend the summer months flying over city and countryside searching for tiny flying insects. True to their name, they nest in chimneys and on the walls of abandoned buildings. Swifts build strange nests of twigs, glued together and attached with their sticky saliva to a wall inside the chimney. They gather in large flocks before migrating to South America for the winter. On a fall evening you might see a tornado-like flock of swifts swirling above a church steeple or large chimney before diving into it at high speed. The whole flock spends the night clinging to the inside vertical walls.

COMMON GRACKLE

SCIENTIFIC NAME: *Quiscalus quiscala*
LENGTH: 12½ in (23 cm)
WINGSPAN: 17 in (43 cm)

Up close, the Common Grackle's plumage shimmers with iridescent blue, purple, and bronze colors, set off by striking yellow eyes and a long, flared tail. From a distance, it just looks solid black. Most Common Grackles live east of the Rocky Mountains. In cities, grackles can be seen strutting across lawns and playing fields searching for insects and seeds or poking into open trashcans. The grackle's song is not a thing of beauty. Its throaty *readle-eek* and high-pitched whistles have been described as sounding like a rusty gate.

GREAT-TAILED GRACKLE

SCIENTIFIC NAME: *Quiscalus mexicanus*
LENGTH: 18 in (46 cm)
WINGSPAN: 23 in (58 cm)

The Great-tailed Grackle looks like a supersized Common Grackle. The male has glossy purple plumage and a huge tail; the female is brownish and about half as big as the male. Great-tailed Grackles live west of the Mississippi River, and they are found from Texas all the way to southern California. In cities, Great-tails often hang out together in parks and other places with large grassy lawns. They stay up late at night, and people who live near a roosting flock often complain about being kept awake by the birds' nonstop whistles, squeals, rattles, and other weird sounds.

BARN SWALLOW

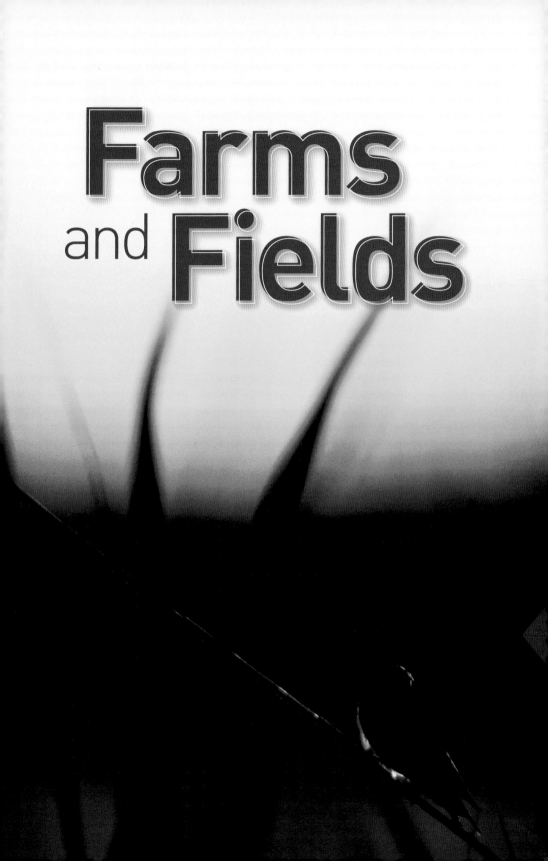

Farms
and Fields

Farms and Fields

HABITAT

DOWNY WOODPECKER

SONG SPARROW

PURPLE MARTIN

LIVING THE COUNTRY LIFE

BALTIMORE ORIOLE

If you are visiting or live in a rural area east of the Rocky Mountains, you don't have to look very hard to see cows, sheep, and horses. But, try being a sharp-eyed bird-watcher and spot the many wild birds that share the land with us. With a little bit of luck and patience you'll find them. Explore the brushy edges of overgrown fields and any nearby woods—these places often have different species. The tall trees around a farmhouse are also good places to look for birds.

RED-SHOULDERED HAWK

GREAT HORNED OWL

EASTERN BLUEBIRD

AMERICAN CROW

WILD TURKEY

BARN SWALLOW

Great Horned Owl

THE GREAT HORNED is the biggest, baddest owl in North America. Its silhouette looks like a barrel-shaped body with "horns." You might see one at dusk or dawn, when it perches in the top of a tree. The "horns" are actually soft feathers that stick up from the top of its head. Some people think those are ears … wrong! An owl has large ear openings hidden under feathers on either side of its head. Like a spy plane, the Great Horned Owl flies on silent wings. It has huge eyes that can see in the dark, and its head is like a radar dish that can swivel 270 degrees. The owl has 3-D hearing that can locate prey hiding under leaves or snow, even when it's pitch-dark out. And not much escapes the clutches of its very sharp talons.

SCIENTIFIC NAME: *Bubo virginianus*
LENGTH: 22 in (56 cm)
WINGSPAN: 44 in (112 cm)

VOICE

Hoots are deep and mellow and often given in a set of five syllables: *hoo hoo-HOO hoooo hoo.* Listen for them calling from the time it gets dark until about midnight, and then again just before sunrise. If you do a good imitation of this owl's call, it might call back to you.

FOOD

The Great Horned Owl's favorite prey is mammals such as mice, rats, opossums, and rabbits, but sometimes they even eat skunks, porcupines, and armadillos! This owl has a very big mouth. Smaller prey get swallowed whole—headfirst, bones and all. If the prey is too big to swallow in one gulp, the owl pulls it apart before eating it.

HABITAT & RANGE

In rural areas, the Great Horned Owl sometimes roosts in the hayloft of an abandoned barn, but it is usually seen perched in a tree. It can live anywhere from the Arctic Circle to the Sonoran Desert, in suburban neighborhoods, or deep in the forest. Only active at night, it spends the day roosting in a tree, unless discovered and mobbed by a gang of crows, its sworn enemies. The Great Horned Owl lives in the same area year-round.

GREAT HORNED OWLS weigh about three to four pounds but can **catch prey** up to about ten pounds—the weight of a house cat!

A CLOSER LOOK

The "horns" are really just soft feathers. The large ears are located lower down.

Huge yellow eyes can spot prey from far away.

Brown plumage with bars and speckles is good camouflage.

Wing feathers have soft edges so that a flying owl is completely silent.

Very sharp talons are used for catching prey.

RANGE MAP KEY

▢ YEAR-ROUND

DOWN THE HATCH . . . AND UP AGAIN!

Owls swallow most of their prey whole—for Great Horned Owls that can be anything up to the size of a small rabbit. Later on, it spits up (regurgitates) a compact pellet of bones and fur, stuff it can't digest.

American Crow

THE AMERICAN CROW is a large black bird that everybody seems to recognize. Often, before you see a flock of crows, you can hear them cawing. If you listen very closely, you will notice different types of caws, depending on what they are communicating to other crows. They might be saying: "All clear, everything's okay" or "Come over here, I found something good to eat" or "DANGER! I see an owl." Crows are bold and intelligent, and when they see something new, they go to investigate. They live in close-knit family flocks. Some "teenaged" birds in the flock act as guards that watch for danger, or as scouts that search for food; others are "mother's helpers" who assist with feeding the nestlings.

SCIENTIFIC NAME: *Corvus brachyrhynchos*
LENGTH: 17½ in (45 cm)
WINGSPAN: 39 in (99 cm)

VOICE

American Crows usually make the harsh cawing sounds *caw, caw, caw, caw*. They also make a "rattle call" that sounds like a fingernail stroking the teeth of a comb and a variety of other calls that send specific messages to other members of their flock. In the East, there's another kind of crow, the Fish Crow. One way to tell them apart is by sound. The Fish Crow says *Uh-uh Uh-uh*.

FOOD

Crows eat an amazing variety of foods—whatever is easiest to get. During the warmer months, they eat insects and earthworms and sometimes prey on the eggs of other birds. Crows will eat mice, young turtles, and human garbage. They also chow down on crops of grains, seeds, nuts, and fruits, which is why farmers invented scarecrows. Winter flocks often rely on finding waste grain that was left in fields after the harvest.

HABITAT & RANGE

There are more than 30 different species of crows in the world. American Crows live all across the United States and in parts of Canada.

CROWS fly in straight lines. The phrase "as the crow flies" means going somewhere by the most **direct** route, just as a crow does.

A CLOSER LOOK

The heavy black bill is a useful tool for grabbing anything edible, from an earthworm on the ground to corn kernels on a corncob, or even for tearing open a garbage bag.

Glossy, black plumage, but it can look paler when the sun reflects off it.

Males and females look identical, but young birds have brownish feathers that are not glossy.

Strong legs and feet for walking on the ground

Farmland and rural areas are especially attractive to crows—they prefer open areas with scattered trees. Winter flocks search out groves of trees where they spend the night together. Most crows that nest in Canada migrate to the United States in winter.

RANGE MAP KEY

- SUMMER (breeding)
- WINTER (nonbreeding)
- YEAR-ROUND

CROWS HATE OWLS

When a flock of crows discovers a sleeping Great Horned Owl (see pp. 62–63) they go crazy—making screeching caws, flying at the owl, and even pecking it (this behavior is called mobbing). If the owl flies off, the crows chase it for long distances. After dark, the tables are turned and the Great Horned Owl goes on the attack. Great Horned Owls kill and eat both adult crows and nestling crows, so it is understandable why crows and owls don't get along.

Barn Swallow

ONE OF THE MOST POPULAR birds of summer, the graceful Barn Swallow swoops over fields and pastures across North America and well beyond its borders. The Barn Swallow is the most widely distributed and abundant swallow in the world. A long, forked tail—it is North America's only swallow with a "swallowtail"— and slender body give it an elegant appearance. In flight, the tail can be spread (when banking or landing) or, more often, folded into a long point. Barn Swallows cruise for insects just a few inches above the ground or over water. Like other swallows, Barn Swallows are often seen perched on telephone wires.

SCIENTIFIC NAME: *Hirundo rustica*
LENGTH: 6¾ in (17 cm)
WINGSPAN: 15 in (38 cm)

VITAL STATISTICS

VOICE

The Barn Swallow's song is a long series of scratchy, warbling phrases, interspersed with a grating rattle. Its flight call is a high-pitched *chee-jit*.

FOOD

Flying insects, including bees, wasps, flying ants, butterflies, and moths are a Barn Swallow's food favorites.

HABITAT & RANGE

Barn Swallows have three basic habitat requirements: open areas for foraging (fields, pastures, golf courses, large yards); a man-made structure to shelter its nest (barn, culvert, bridge, pier, porch); and a body of water that provides mud for nest building. They avoid deserts and dense forest. Most Barn Swallows that nest in North America fly all the way to Central or South America for the winter. These birds live on all the world's continents, except chilly Antarctica where there are almost no flying insects to eat.

BARN SWALLOWS are very graceful fliers that can easily **swoop** through an open barn door to reach their nest and **feed their young.**

A CLOSER LOOK

Females have shorter tails than males, and young birds have very short tails.

A long, forked tail helps the Barn Swallow make tight turns and dives.

Although its bill is small, the Barn Swallow has a wide mouth that helps it catch flying insects as large as moths and butterflies.

Glossy, blue back and reddish brown throat

RANGE MAP KEY

- SUMMER (breeding)
- WINTER (nonbreeding)
- MIGRATION
- YEAR-ROUND

GIMME SHELTER

A nesting platform added to a porch or open garage is a good place for Barn Swallows to build their nest of mud and straw. Nowadays, they rarely nest anywhere other than in or on a man-made building. Before people built houses, barns, and bridges, Barn Swallows nested in caves.

Eastern Bluebird

EASTERN BLUEBIRDS have beautiful colors and millions of adoring fans. For hundreds of years, poems and songs like "The Bluebird of Happiness" have been written about them, and it's considered good luck to see one. In fact, they are the official state bird of both Missouri and New York. Fifty years ago, bluebirds were in trouble. Introduced species such as European Starlings and House Sparrows had taken over the nest holes that bluebirds needed to raise their families. But people came to the rescue and put up millions of nest boxes just for bluebirds, designed to keep those other birds out. Sometimes the bluebird houses are evenly spaced along a fence or country road that borders a field—this is called a "bluebird trail."

SCIENTIFIC NAME: *Sialia sialis*
LENGTH: 7 in (18 cm)
WINGSPAN: 13 in (33 cm)

VOICE

Eastern Bluebirds have a simple musical song that consists of a rich warble: *chur chur-lee chur-lee*. Males trying to attract a mate often sing from a high perch or even while in flight. After they start to nest, they are much quieter.

FOOD

From spring to early fall, bluebirds feast on insects. To hunt for an insect, a bluebird perches on a fence or low branch and stares at the ground looking for any movement. When it spies something it quickly flies down and grabs it in its bill. In winter, when insects are hard to find, bluebirds eat lots of berries and small fruits.

HABITAT & RANGE

If you live east of the Rocky Mountains in an area with open fields and trees, chances are you have Eastern Bluebirds as neighbors. They are usually easy to spot because they like to perch on fences and low branches, right out in the open. As you ride home from school, look for a flash of brilliant blue along the roadside—it's probably Mr. or Ms. Bluebird. Most of the bluebirds that nest in Canada and the Upper Midwest migrate to warmer southern areas for the winter.

TO SEE bluebirds up close, try feeding them mealworms. Put live **mealworms** in a shallow bowl outside in the morning and evening.

A CLOSER LOOK

The small, dark bill is good for catching insects but not strong enough to chisel a nest hole into a tree trunk. That's why bluebirds have to nest in an old woodpecker hole or a man-made birdhouse.

Large, dark eyes are good at spotting insects on the ground, even from far away.

The male has deep blue upper parts and a warm reddish brown breast; the colors are paler and grayer in the female. Juvenile bluebirds have spots.

Males

RANGE MAP KEY

- SUMMER (breeding)
- WINTER (nonbreeding)
- YEAR-ROUND

LOOK AT ME

A male Eastern Bluebird works hard to find a mate. First he stakes a claim to a birdhouse or nest cavity and defends it from all others. Then, he brings nest material to the hole and constantly goes in and out. To make sure any nearby females see him, he flashes his blue wings, holding one wing high in the air and then the other. After mating, the female builds the nest and incubates the eggs.

Mini-Profiles

FARMS AND FIELDS

Some birds need more space than others. Farm fields and woodlots offer great places for birds to nest and find food. See if you can spot one of these birds when you're out in wide-open spaces.

WILD TURKEY

SCIENTIFIC NAME: *Meleagris gallopavo*
LENGTH: male 46 in (117 cm); female 37 in (94 cm)
WINGSPAN: male 64 in (163 cm); female 50 in (127 cm)

The turkey we like to eat at Thanksgiving is the farm-raised version of a wild bird still roaming the fields and forests of North America. The Aztec were already raising turkeys for food when the Spanish conquistadores arrived, and domesticated turkeys were soon shipped back to Europe. Today, turkeys are farmed around the world. The unusual bare skin of the wild turkey's head is colored blue and red, and its chunky body is cloaked in coppery brown feathers. Small flocks walk on the ground searching for nuts, berries, and insects to eat, and then fly up into a tree to spend the night in safety. Benjamin Franklin wanted the Wild Turkey to be our national bird, but was outvoted by supporters of the Bald Eagle.

RED-SHOULDERED HAWK

SCIENTIFIC NAME: *Buteo lineatus*
LENGTH: 17 in (43 cm)
WINGSPAN: 40 in (102 cm)

Large and boldly colored, the Red-shouldered Hawk is common in rural and suburban parts of the eastern United States and also in California. Pretty, reddish brown feathers on its shoulders (where the wing bends) contrast with its tail of black and white bands. Listen in spring for a pair of courting Red-shoulders to loudly proclaim their territory—screaming *KEE-ahh* back and forth to each other—while circling high above the forest. They like to nest in woods near a stream or river where they can hunt for small mammals, frogs, snakes, and lizards.

DOWNY WOODPECKER

SCIENTIFIC NAME: *Picoides pubescens*
LENGTH: 6¾ in (17 cm)
WINGSPAN: 12 in (30 cm)

The tiny Downy Woodpecker—the smallest woodpecker in North America—is common from Maine to California. The most likely woodpecker to show up at a bird feeder, the Downy especially enjoys eating suet (animal fat, usually mixed with seeds or fruit). Like most woodpeckers, it is black and white, although the male has a spot of bright red on the back of his head. The Downy is small enough to search for food on thin branches and weed stems which wouldn't be able to support the Downy's larger but very similar looking cousin, the Hairy Woodpecker. The Downy's call is a sharp, high-pitched *pik!*

PURPLE MARTIN

SCIENTIFIC NAME: *Progne subis*
LENGTH: 8 in (20 cm)
WINGSPAN: 18 in (46 cm)

Purple Martins are insect-eating machines that catch their prey in flight—everything from dragonflies to tiny midges. Contrary to popular belief, mosquitoes are rarely on the menu because they fly too low. Martins love the company of other martins. In the East they only nest in man-made martin houses—apartments that can hold 20 or more families—or hollow gourds hung in groups. They may squabble over the best locations, but they rarely nest alone. The males are deep purple-black and the females are similar but have pale bellies. In the fall, they form huge flocks that stay together until they reach their winter home in the Amazon.

SONG SPARROW

SCIENTIFIC NAME: *Melospiza melodia*
LENGTH: 6 in (15 cm)
WINGSPAN: 8¼ in (21 cm)

If you see a small, brown bird with streaks poking around your backyard or along the brushy edges of a field, consider the Song Sparrow first—it's the most common sparrow in North America. Take a look at the streaks on the center of its breast, which usually come together to form a larger spot or "stickpin." In spring and summer, the male proclaims his territory from an eye-level perch by singing a loud and musical song that ends in a trill. Song Sparrows living in backyards and around farms often become quite tame, especially if you scatter birdseed on the ground for them.

BALTIMORE ORIOLE

SCIENTIFIC NAME: *Icterus galbula*
LENGTH: 8¼ in (21 cm)
WINGSPAN: 11½ in (29 cm)

A flash of orange in the top of a large shade tree, the sound of loud, flute-like whistles, or the sight of a woven nest drooping from the tip of a high branch are all signs that a pair of Baltimore Orioles are living nearby. Through a pair of binoculars, the male is a tropical-looking fireball of orange and black, and the female is only slightly less colorful. The Baltimore Oriole is the official state bird of Maryland, which is, of course, also the home of the Baltimore Orioles baseball team.

BROWN PELICAN

Beach
and Bay

Beach and Bay

HABITAT

CASPIAN TERN

SANDERLING

RUDDY TURNSTONE

SURF SCOTER

BIRDS LOVE THE SEASHORE

You'll always see a few gulls and sandpipers loafing on a sandy beach, but if you want to see birds in action—and lots of them—check out a nearby salt marsh or quiet bay. Birds are always on the lookout for a meal and those are places where they can find lots to eat.

HERRING GULL

OSPREY

AMERICAN OYSTERCATCHER

BROWN PELICAN

COMMON LOON

BLACK SKIMMER

Brown Pelican

PELICANS ARE GREAT FUN to watch when you're at the beach. A group of them will fly low over the water until they spot a school of fish near the surface. Then, after gaining some altitude, they tuck their wings in and dive straight down into the water, emerging a moment later with a bulging pouch . . . if they're successful. When not on the wing, they spend hours loafing on a dock, jetty, or sandy beach. The Brown Pelican was listed as an endangered species in 1970, its population depleted by hunting and pollution. But conservation measures, especially the banning of a pesticide called DDT, were so successful that the birds were taken off the list in 2009, and there are more pelicans now than there have ever been.

SCIENTIFIC NAME: *Pelecanus occidentalis*
LENGTH: 48 in (122 cm)
WINGSPAN: 84 in (213 cm)

VOICE

Pelicans rarely make any sounds except at the breeding colony. There the adults have low, hoarse calls. The nestlings keep up a steady squawking chorus, demanding to be fed.

FOOD

Fish, fish, and more fish, from tiny sardines to fish as large as mackerel. Sometimes when a pelican has a full pouch, a gull will reach in and steal a fish before the pelican can swallow it.

HABITAT & RANGE

The Brown Pelican is found close to warm seashore environments, but pelicans do visit southern California's salty Salton Sea located in the desert, more than 100 miles from the ocean. They build their nests in short trees, shrubs, or on the ground. They tend to gather in colonies when nesting, often with other species such as gulls or herons. On the Atlantic coast, their nesting grounds are mainly on small islands covered with low-growing vegetation. The Channel Islands off southern California are home to

DURING a dive, the pelican **folds** back its wings so they won't break, and it hits the water bill-first.

A CLOSER LOOK

The pouch is made of "rubbery" skin that can balloon out to hold more than three gallons of water and fish.

Even the pelican's eyes can change color. Nobody is sure why, but they go from white to brown when nesting.

Usually the pelican's neck is brown, but in winter it changes to white.

Its long toes are completely webbed, so swimming is a breeze. When landing on the water the pelican uses its huge feet as skids to help it stop.

Pelicans are heavyweight birds, weighing about eight pounds.

many nesting pelicans because there are few people and lots of perfect spots to nest. In summer, some birds wander to the north.

RANGE MAP KEY

SUMMER (breeding)

MIGRATION

YEAR-ROUND

A BILL AND A POUCH

A good fisherman needs good equipment, and Mother Nature has provided the pelican with some great gear—a really long bill with an amazing pouch of rubbery skin that can expand to hold gallons of water... and fish. As a pelican dives from the air into a school of fish, its pouch balloons open underwater, trapping both fish and water. Then the pelican comes to the surface, strains the water out of its pouch, and swallows the fish that are inside. Sashimi anyone?

Osprey

THE YELLOW-EYED OSPREY is the only North American hawk whose diet is almost 100 percent fresh fish. These birds have powerful wings that, over a 20-year life span, might carry the bird more than 160,000 miles on migration. They build big nests of sticks high up on treetops, power poles, or in some cases on tall platforms provided by people. Generations of Ospreys will use the same nesting site, adding more sticks to it year after year. Once its nestlings have hatched, the Osprey carries its still squirming prey back to its nest, held firmly by sturdy claws. The Osprey's eggs don't all hatch at the same time. The first chick to hatch is the biggest and strongest, and often demands and gets more attention and food than the younger babies.

SCIENTIFIC NAME: *Pandion haliaetus*
LENGTH: 24 in (61 cm)
WINGSPAN: 63 in (160 cm)

VITAL STATISTICS

VOICE

The Osprey's voice is surprisingly high-pitched for such a large bird. Their call is a series of chirps that are spaced out: *eeee—eeee—eeee*. When they are alarmed, the chirps are closer together and rise in intensity; this may happen when an unfamiliar Osprey is approaches the nest.

FOOD

Ospreys eat fish. Period. Over 80 species of fresh- and saltwater fish have been counted among their catches. The largest recorded fish caught was about $2\frac{1}{2}$ pounds, but most fish weigh between $\frac{1}{3}$ to $\frac{2}{3}$ pound. When it is carrying a fish in its feet, the Osprey lines the fish up headfirst in the wind to reduce drag—it looks like the Osprey is toting a torpedo.

HABITAT & RANGE

Ospreys live around rivers, small and medium-size lakes, reservoirs, lagoons, bays, and salt marshes. Look for them flying over the water, or perched in a tall tree or on top of a power or telephone pole or cell phone tower.

OSPREYS' stick nests are big enough for a **person** to sit in.

A CLOSER LOOK

Yellow eyes can correct for the distortion of the water and guide an osprey directly to a fish. Young ospreys have orange eyes.

Bold, dark eye stripe probably reduces glare off the water so Ospreys can better see beneath the surface.

Huge talons—four on each foot—and feet with rough, spiny bottoms make it impossible for a fish to escape once caught.

Strong wings measure about five feet from tip to tip.

Most Ospreys leave North America by late fall. Many migrate as far south as South America. Ospreys live around the world.

RANGE MAP KEY

▢ SUMMER (breeding)		▢ WINTER (nonbreeding)
▢ MIGRATION		▢ YEAR-ROUND

HIGH-DIVING CHAMP

Drawing a bead on a fish near the surface, this Osprey is unlikely to miss. With the style and accuracy of an Olympic diver, this big hawk isn't afraid to get a little wet—its dives can take it completely underwater. Its wings are folded back so that its bones don't break when it hits the water.

Herring Gull

HERRING GULLS are sturdy gray birds with pure white heads, yellow bills with a red spot at the tip, and pinkish legs. In winter, they can be found along all of North America's coastlines, and they are year-round residents from the mid-Atlantic north to Canada, and around the Great Lakes. In spring, many Herring Gulls migrate to northern Canada to nest. They can handle almost any kind of weather, and they can survive on most any kind of food they can find or steal from others. Some birds live in wild places and might follow foraging whales or dolphins to feed on small fish that are driven to the surface. But Herring Gulls don't mind being around people, and some birds seem to spend their entire lives hanging out around beach resorts and marinas.

SCIENTIFIC NAME: *Larus argentatus*
LENGTH: 25 in (64 cm)
WINGSPAN: 58 in (147 cm)

VOICE

Herring Gulls have a variety of calls, from a quiet *mew* to a sharp *ha-ha-ha-ha!* and trumpeting *keeyow, kyow-kyow-kyow.* If you have spent time near the ocean, you have probably memorized not just the sound of the crashing waves, but also the insistent calling of the gulls.

FOOD

Herring Gulls are omnivores—they gobble down just about anything, from shellfish to small fish and squid to worms and bugs. These birds aren't squeamish about eating at a garbage dump or squabbling for french fries from beachgoers either. They also scavenge for dead fish and other animals. Herring Gulls will raid the nests of other birds and eat their eggs and chicks, and some male Herring Gulls will even eat the chicks of neighboring Herring Gulls.

HABITAT & RANGE

Herring Gulls can be found in lots of different places, such as beaches, lakes, rivers, and mudflats. They are almost always in a location that has water nearby. In winter, they tend to hang out in groups—large flocks are often seen around garbage dumps and landfills.

A YOUNG Herring Gull's plumage is all brown and **speckled.** It takes about 3½ years before a young bird looks like an adult.

A CLOSER LOOK

Gulls can drink seawater because they have a gland behind the bill that extracts the salt and lets the super salty liquid drip from the nostril.

The heavy bill has a hooked tip that can deal with many types of food—dead or alive.

Long wings allow a gull to soar without much flapping.

Like all other gulls, Herring Gulls have webbed feet and are good swimmers.

Adult

Pink legs are the color of bubblegum.

In summer, they nest in colonies on islands, barrier beaches, and elevated marshy areas where they can keep an eye out for predators. Herring Gulls are more common on the East Coast than the West Coast.

RANGE MAP KEY

- SUMMER (breeding)
- MIGRATION
- WINTER (nonbreeding)
- YEAR-ROUND

CLAMMING IT UP

Ever tried to open a hard-shell clam? It isn't easy, even with a special tool. But that hasn't stopped Herring Gulls from eating these tasty morsels. Their solution: grab the clam in your bill, fly high in the air, aim for some rocks (or a paved road), and let go. If the clam doesn't crack to smithereens on the first drop, keep on trying.

Black Skimmer

THE BLACK SKIMMER is an unusual waterbird—its knife-like red-and-black bill is much longer on the lower half than the upper, a feature that fits its feeding method. The skimmer flies just above the water's surface with its long wings flapping high above its body, and its lower bill slicing through the water. When its lower bill touches a small fish, the upper bill snaps down, trapping the fish, which it then swallows. Because it finds its prey by touch, some Black Skimmers hunt at night when fish often swim closer to the surface. Skimmers are often seen in flocks, and they nest in colonies. Most types of North American birds have many close relatives, but the Black Skimmer has only two other relatives on the planet: one in Africa and another in India.

SCIENTIFIC NAME: *Rynchops niger*
LENGTH: 18 in (46 cm)
WINGSPAN: 44 in (112 cm)

VOICE

The hollow, nasal laughing *k'wukk waak* sound made by the Black Skimmer might remind you of a low-pitched squeaker toy that your dog enjoys playing with, or a honking bicycle horn. A flock of skimmers calling to each other makes a chuckling chorus.

FOOD

Black Skimmers eat fish and sometimes travel as much as five miles from their colony in search of good places to skim for them. Since they swallow their prey whole, they can manage fish only up to five inches long—herring, mullet, and pipefish are among their favorites. They also may eat a few small crabs and shrimp.

HABITAT & RANGE

Black Skimmers nest on sandy or shell beaches and skim for fish in quiet lagoons, harbors, and bays. They have also colonized the Salton Sea, a salty inland lake in the desert near Los Angeles, California. Much of their coastal habitat has had houses built along it, but artificial islands that have been built out of the sand and mud dredged out of harbors and marinas have become important nesting sites for skimmers. They are year-round residents in southern California, the Gulf Coast, and southern Atlantic beaches. Skimmers are also found in Central and South America.

WITH THIS VIEW of the Black Skimmer's bill, you can see how it earned **nicknames** like "Cut-Water," "Knifebill," and "Scissorbill."

A CLOSER LOOK

Long wings allow the skimmer to fly just inches above the water.

Black-and-white plumage is very striking.

Just the lower, longer part of the bill slices through the water.

The pupils of the skimmer's eyes can narrow down into vertical slits, which reduces the glare off the water, like a built-in pair of sunglasses.

The tip of its bright red bill is black. The black pigment in the bill makes it stronger and less likely to beak if the bill hits an underwater rock while skimming.

RANGE MAP KEY

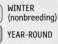

■ SUMMER (breeding)	□ WINTER (nonbreeding)
□ MIGRATION	■ YEAR-ROUND

WHEN I GROW UP . . .

Looking totally unlike its parent, a baby skimmer has a lot of growing to do. Its fluffy plumage looks just like the sand, so predators won't see it (camouflage), and its nest is just a shallow, hollowed-out area with nothing added to it. When it hatches, its bill is short and the upper and lower parts are equal in length. Within four weeks the lower part is already longer, but it take months to grow to full-size.

Mini-Profiles
BEACH AND BAY

Beaches and coastal marshes are food factories for birds that eat fish and marine invertebrates like crabs, shellfish, and worms. Next time you're by the beach or bay, look for these birds.

SURF SCOTER

SCIENTIFIC NAME: *Melanitta perspicillata*
LENGTH: 20 in (51 cm)
WINGSPAN: 30 in (76 cm)

The male Surf Scoter is a black-and-white sea duck with a colorful bill; the female is dark brown with white patches on her head. Scoters spend the winter up and down the Pacific and Atlantic coasts, in bays and estuaries. They feed on mollusks (clams and mussels) and crustaceans (mostly crabs). Some immature scoters remain at the seashore all summer while the adults fly to freshwater lakes in the Arctic tundra to nest. Sometimes, the tundra lakes get so crowded that mother scoters lose track of their own chicks and feed someone else's babies. No one seems to mind.

COMMON LOON

SCIENTIFIC NAME: *Gavia immer*
LENGTH: 32 in (81 cm)
WINGSPAN: 46 in (117 cm)

Loons are known for their weird yodeling call, which some people think is creepy when they first hear it. Most of their yodeling is done in summer on lakes in the northern U.S. and Canada where they nest. The rest of the year is usually spent in coastal areas, around bays and harbors. The Common Loon has huge webbed feet that propel it during dives in pursuit of the fish it feeds on. When a fish is caught, it's often swallowed underwater. You may see a loon swimming along with just its head underwater—"snorkeling"—while it's looking for a fish to chase after.

AMERICAN OYSTERCATCHER

SCIENTIFIC NAME: *Haematopus palliatus*
LENGTH: 18½ in (47 cm)
WINGSPAN: 34 in (86 cm)

It's impossible not to notice the eye-catching American Oystercatcher with its large lipstick-red bill. These big shorebirds of the Atlantic and Gulf coasts often gather in small flocks at the best feeding locations: salt marshes, mudflats, and shellfish beds exposed at low tide. It uses its long, stout bill to probe for food and pry it open. Mussels, clams, oysters, crabs, and marine worms are all on the menu. On the Pacific coast, you may see the American Oystercatcher's close cousin, the Black Oystercatcher. Its plumage is completely black and it prefers rocky coastlines, but it has the same bright red bill.

RUDDY TURNSTONE

SCIENTIFIC NAME: *Arenaria interpres*
LENGTH: 9½ in (24 cm)
WINGSPAN: 21 in (53 cm)

Turnstones are short-legged, chunky-looking shorebirds named for their habit of flipping over stones, shells, and bits of seaweed with their pointed bills while searching for food. Social birds, they gather together in small flocks, chattering as they feed along rocky shores and pebbly beaches. Bold markings on the turnstone's wings, back, and tail are hard to miss when it flies. Like many shorebirds, turnstones nest in the Arctic, but spend most of the year on the seacoast and even around the Great Lakes.

SANDERLING

SCIENTIFIC NAME: *Calidris alba*
LENGTH: 8 in (20 cm)
WINGSPAN: 17 in (43 cm)

During most of the year, flocks of Sanderlings can be found at the surf's edge on beaches, up and down the Atlantic and Pacific coasts. They hang out on the same sandy beaches that people enjoy, but the Sanderlings are there for a reason—food. These pale little shorebirds that seem to be chasing after waves are actually running to where the sand is wet and probing for small animals to eat. To nest, Sanderlings fly to the Arctic tundra for a few short months, but they spend the rest of the year at the beach … sweet.

CASPIAN TERN

SCIENTIFIC NAME: *Hydroprogne caspia*
LENGTH: 21 in (53 cm)
WINGSPAN: 50 in (127 cm)

The Caspian Tern is the biggest tern in the world—as big as a gull—with a thick red bill and black wing tips. Like many other terns, the Caspian cruises high over the water searching for something to eat. When a fish is spotted, the Caspian dives in headfirst to grab dinner in its bill. Coastal salt marshes, barrier islands, and islands in rivers and lakes are prime locations for a breeding colony. Nesting terns are very aggressive about defending their eggs and young from predators and people, so stay clear or risk getting dive-bombed. Young terns—even when fully grown—seem to have a difficult time growing up and learning to catch fish. They follow their parents around for months loudly begging for a free meal.

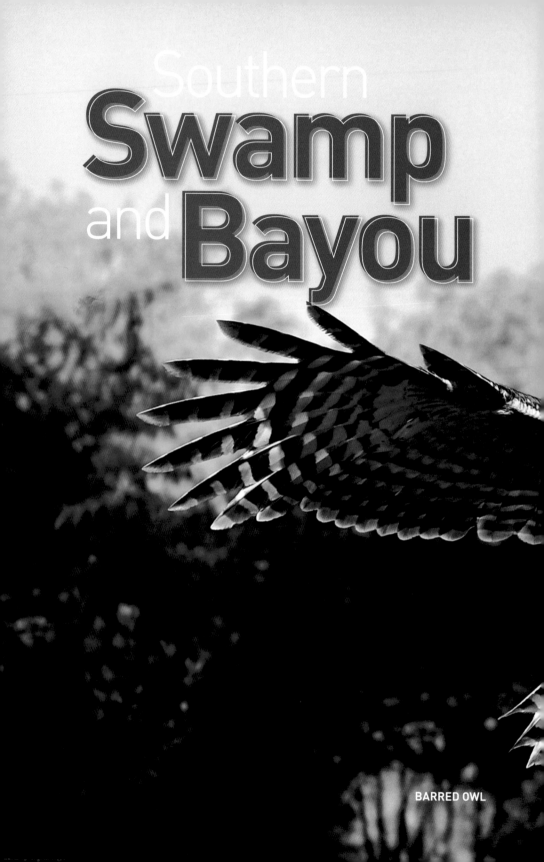

Southern
Swamp
and Bayou

BARRED OWL

Southern Swamp and Bayou

HABITAT

SWALLOW-TAILED KITE

ANHINGA

PURPLE GALLINULE

A UNIQUE PLACE TO LIVE

A swamp is a low-lying wooded area that is usually flooded with overflow from a nearby river or lake, and is full of plant and animal life. Tupelo, cypress, and other types of trees and vegetation get lots of water and grow lush. Bayous, found along the Gulf Coast, can be a slow-moving river or stream, or a marshy lake or wetland. Many types of animals—crayfish, shrimp, catfish, alligators, frogs, and a great variety of insects—are abundant in swamps and bayous, and so are the birds that feed on them.

BARRED OWL

PILEATED WOODPECKER

YELLOW-CROWNED NIGHT-HERON

PROTHONOTARY WARBLER

SNOWY EGRET

WOOD DUCK

LIMPKIN

Snowy Egret

SNOWY EGRETS, WITH THEIR ELEGANT look, brilliant white plumage, and long, graceful legs are common in many wetland areas, but they were almost wiped out during the late 19th century. They were hunted for their beautiful white feathers, which were used to decorate women's hats. The Snowy Egret was saved by the efforts of early conservationists who started the Audubon Society in order to stop the killing of birds for the millinery (hat-making) trade. There are other species of all-white egrets, but you can identify a Snowy by its medium size, thin black bill, black legs, and yellow feet. Snowy Egrets may have small eyes, but their eyesight is excellent and helps them spot food.

SCIENTIFIC NAME: *Egretta thula*
LENGTH: 24 in (61 cm)
WINGSPAN: 41 in (104 cm)

VOICE

Snowy Egrets are usually silent. When disturbed or agitated they make a variety of harsh croaks and other sounds, like someone clearing their throat or gargling.

FOOD

These birds are active—sometimes frantic—foragers in shallow water. They search for fish, insects, frogs, snakes and lizards. They also eat aquatic invertebrates (animals without backbones living in water) like shrimp, crayfish, and crabs. Some of their food lives in fresh water, some in salt water, and some in brackish swamps, but to Snowy Egrets, they're all good.

HABITAT & RANGE

Snowy Egrets are found in many kinds of watery places—fresh- and saltwater marshes, sheltered bays and lagoons, ponds and bayous. They like to raise their families in groups (colonies), often building their nests of sticks in trees or shrubs near the water, or sometimes on the ground in marshy areas. In winter, northern birds leave areas where marshes

WHEN courting, long **curling** plumes grow from a Snowy Egret's back, the skin on its face turns red, and its feet turn orange.

A CLOSER LOOK

Long black legs allow the Snowy to wade out to where its favorite food lives.

Black bill with a fine tip for grabbing minnows and small crustaceans, such as crayfish and shrimp

Yellow feet attract the small minnows that the Snowy eats.

Long neck, usually held in an S-curve, can uncoil in a flash when the Snowy strikes at a fish.

and ponds freeze over. Snowy Egrets also live in Central and South America.

RANGE MAP KEY

SUMMER (breeding)	WINTER (nonbreeding)
MIGRATION	YEAR-ROUND

MAGICAL GOLDEN SLIPPERS

This egret's yellow feet ("golden slippers") are more than just an easy way for people to identify it. Small fish and minnows—the Snowy's favorite food—are actually attracted to their color and movement. When a minnow comes by to investigate, it's like having takeout dinner delivered to the door. The Snowy also uses those magic feet to stir up the mud and scare hidden prey into view.

Anhinga

THE ANHINGA is a large diving bird with a long neck, often seen along the edges of slow-moving streams and bayous in the American South and along the Gulf Coast. It can swim underwater with only its head and long, snake-like neck showing above the surface. The Anhinga's heavy bones and nonwaterproof feathers allow it to swim underwater with ease as it stalks fish. But wet feathers can't keep the Anhinga warm, so it spends long periods of time perched on a log with outstretched wings trying to dry off. The Anhinga is also a graceful flier and can stay aloft for long periods of time soaring on the air currents.

SCIENTIFIC NAME: *Anhinga anhinga*
LENGTH: 35 in (89 cm)
WINGSPAN: 45 in (114 cm)

VOICE

Usually silent, except during breeding season. Around their nest site, Anhingas make harsh and grating noises that sound like radio static.

FOOD

The Anhinga's favorite food is medium-size fish, including bass, mullet, pickerel, sunfish, sucker, and gizzard shad. If there aren't enough fish, the Anhinga will eat insects, crayfish, shrimp, and even snakes, baby alligators, frogs, and small turtles.

HABITAT & RANGE

Anhingas are aquatic birds, usually found in or near shallow, freshwater streams, cypress swamps, ponds, and marshy areas. They prefer locations with overhanging trees or fallen logs, where they can sit in the sun to warm up and dry their wings. Anhingas sometimes forage in brackish lagoons or tidal streams. They breed in colonies with other waterbirds, such as herons, egrets, ibises, storks, and cormorants. Most Anhingas don't migrate, but live in the same place year-round. They also live in Mexico and in Central and South America.

BABY ANHINGAS have downy white feathers and cannot fly until they are about two months old.

A CLOSER LOOK

During courtship, the male Anhinga's face turns brilliant green and blue.

Male's plumage is black with silvery spots and streaks; the female has a light brown neck and breast.

Female

The long, sharp bill is used to spear fish.

Huge webbed feet propel the Anhinga underwater.

The long tail has curious ridges running across it.

RANGE MAP KEY

- SUMMER (breeding)
- MIGRATION
- YEAR-ROUND

THE FISH DON'T STAND A CHANCE

Cruising underwater, the Anhinga searches for fish in shallow, weedy areas. Its neck bones have a special built-in hinge and muscles that allows it to thrust its daggerlike bill forward—like a lightning-fast speargun. Fish are usually impaled through the side with a partially open bill, which has backward-facing barbs so that the fish won't slip off. To eat, the fish is taken to the surface, flipped in the air, caught headfirst, and swallowed whole.

93

Barred Owl

THE RICH MELLOW hooting call of the Barred Owl is commonly heard in southern swampland. This large owl is found in dense woodland all over the eastern half of the U.S. and in the Pacific Northwest. Almost as big as a Great Horned Owl (see pp. 62–63), the Barred Owl has a round head and no ear tufts. Though it is well camouflaged, the Barred Owl tends to fly away when its roost is approached, unless it lives in an area where people frequently pass by, for example, near a boardwalk in a swamp. In those situations, people are not perceived as a threat, and the owl will stay put and be easy to get a good look at. The Barred Owl is aggressive in defending its territory, but not as aggressive as the Great Horned Owl.

SCIENTIFIC NAME: *Strix varia*
LENGTH: 21 in (53 cm)
WINGSPAN: 42 in (107 cm)

VOICE

The Barred Owl is more often heard than seen. Its unique call is heard during the day more than any other owl's, and is easy to recognize: "who-cooks-for-you, who-cooks-for-YOU-ALL." The Barred Owl is often called "the eight-hooter," with its last hoot trailing downward. If you imitate its call, it may answer you.

FOOD

Because they have excellent hearing and night vision, Barred Owls are able to hunt at night. They catch and eat small mammals like mice, squirrels, and rabbits, but they also eat birds, snakes, lizards, frogs, fish, and large insects. In southern swamps, the Barred Owl's belly feathers can turn pink from eating lots of crayfish.

HABITAT & RANGE

Barred Owls live in forests with large trees and lots of them. They are especially common in forested river bottoms and southern swamps, but they also

BARRED OWLS sometimes **hunt** during the day, especially if the weather is cloudy or snowy.

A CLOSER LOOK

Hooked, yellow bill (the large mouth that can swallow a whole mouse is hidden by feathers).

Huge, dark brown eyes that see well at night

Mostly brown plumage is spotted with white above and pale buff below with dark, vertical streaks—great camouflage when perched close to a tree trunk.

Disk of feathers around the face helps to funnel sound to the ears located underneath.

Wing feathers have soft edges so that flight is silent and won't scare off a potential meal.

reside in wooded suburbs and even in large city parks. Barred Owls nest in a natural tree cavity or reuse the open nest of another large bird such as a hawk or crow. These birds don't migrate, but their range is expanding.

RANGE MAP KEY

YEAR-ROUND

OWL WARS

The population of Spotted Owls (left) that lives in the Pacific Northwest is protected by the Endangered Species Act. Protecting the Spotted Owls' old-growth forest habitat from being logged may not be enough, however. Turns out that Barred Owls—the Spotted Owl's closest relatives—have been moving into the area for decades and are driving out the less aggressive Spotted Owls. Should people intervene or should we let nature take its course? There don't seem to be any easy answers.

Wood Duck

ALTHOUGH the Wood Duck looks like it could be a brightly painted wooden duck, it is named for its habitat choice—heavily wooded swamps and streams. They are one of the few ducks that can perch in trees, and they also nest in tree cavities. Male Wood Ducks have breathtaking colors in complicated patterns, and both males and females have bushy crests that make their heads look large and rounded. During the late 19th century, when Wood Duck populations were declining rapidly due to habitat loss and commercial hunting, some ornithologists worried that the Wood Duck would become extinct. But remote southern swamps offered the Wood Duck a safe haven. A federal ban on the hunting of Wood Ducks was enacted in 1918 and lasted until 1941 and, over time, the population recovered.

SCIENTIFIC NAME: *Aix sponsa*
LENGTH: 18½ in (47 cm)
WINGSPAN: 30 in (76 cm)

VOICE

Female Wood Ducks make a high-pitched *ooo-eeek ooo-eeek!* when disturbed or taking flight. Males have a thin, rising and falling whistle, *zeeet!*

FOOD

Wood Ducks are able to forage in water, on land, and in trees. They eat water plants and grasses, tree seeds and acorns, wild berries, grapes and cherries, and wheat, corn, and rice left in harvested fields. In summer, ducklings eat lots of insects and tiny animals, such as snails, because they need high-protein foods to grow.

HABITAT & RANGE

Wood Ducks do well in many watery places. Swamps and marshes work best for them, but wooded creeks, streams, and small rivers are also important breeding areas. Beaver ponds, with lots of vegetation and nearby trees, are ideal. They prefer to nest in natural tree cavities but sometimes use an old squirrel or Pileated Wood-pecker nest hole. Nest boxes put up by people are also very popular.

WOOD DUCK ducklings are unable to fly until about two months old, but they **feed** themselves from the very start.

A CLOSER LOOK

In good light, the male's dark colors light up with blue, green, and bronze highlights.

Male

Unlike most ducks, Wood Ducks have strong claws for perching on branches.

The female has browner colors—better for camouflage—and a teardrop-shaped eye patch.

Female

Wood Ducks that breed in the north migrate south for the winter. Their only close relative, the Mandarin Duck, lives in Japan and China.

RANGE MAP KEY

- SUMMER (breeding)
- WINTER (nonbreeding)
- YEAR-ROUND

BABIES THAT BOUNCE

The day that a baby Wood Duck hatches, it faces a huge challenge. It's in a nest hole perhaps 50 or more feet off the ground, and Mom is on the ground calling to her family to join her. Problem is, ducklings can't fly, so the only way down is to jump. Fortunately, ducklings are lightweight balls of fluff that usually just bounce off the ground unhurt. Once the whole family has made it, they stick close to Mom and she leads them to water.

Mini-Profiles

SOUTHERN SWAMP AND BAYOU

Few people live in swamps, but for many birds, a swamp is a paradise full of food and a safe place to nest and raise a family. These birds may not be easy to spot, but keep your eyes peeled—you never know what you'll see.

YELLOW-CROWNED NIGHT-HERON

SCIENTIFIC NAME: *Nyctanassa violacea*
LENGTH: 24 in (61 cm)
WINGSPAN: 42 in (107 cm)

Yellow-crowned Night-Herons have a favorite food—crabs, which they hunt with slow, stalking movements in the swampy wetlands, marshes, and bayous where they live. When a large crab is caught, the Yellow-crowned Night-Heron slowly tears it apart and devours it, body first. The two species are so tied together that the timing of the Yellow-crowned's breeding cycle is determined by the availability of enough crabs, although the secretive Yellow-crowned also eats crayfish, insects, small fish, and frogs, when living in inland freshwater locations.

SWALLOW-TAILED KITE

SCIENTIFIC NAME: *Elanoides forficatus*
LENGTH: 23 in (58 cm)
WINGSPAN: 48 in (122 cm)

One of the most graceful fliers in the bird world, the Swallow-tailed Kite soars high on a rising hot air (called a thermal), swoops low in a stiff breeze, and cruises over tree-filled swamps and bayous, all while searching for large flying insects to snatch up and eat on the wing. It also drops down on snakes, lizards, and frogs. The Swallow-tailed Kite has a white head and belly, black back and wings, and a long forked tail that moves constantly in flight, helping to make turns and maneuver in the sky. It breeds along the Gulf Coast, in Florida, and as far north as South Carolina; it winters in South America.

PURPLE GALLINULE

SCIENTIFIC NAME: *Porphyrio martinica*
LENGTH: 13 in (33 cm)
WINGSPAN: 22 in (56 cm)

The brightly colored Purple Gallinule is nicknamed the "Southern Lily Pad Chicken" or the "Swamp Hen" because of its size and shape—not because it is related to the kind of chickens that are on our dinner tables. Long yellow legs that end in very long and slender toes allow the Purple Gallinule to stride across the vegetation-covered surface of a pond or swampy area while searching for food. An omnivore, it will eat the leaves, seeds, and fruits of a variety of plants growing in the water or on land; it also devours insects, snakes, frogs, spiders, worms, and fish, and the eggs and young of other birds. Newly hatched chicks are fed by their parents as well as by up to eight "helpers" who are usually the older siblings.

LIMPKIN

SCIENTIFIC NAME: *Aramus guarauna*
LENGTH: 26 in (66 cm)
WINGSPAN: 40 in (102 cm)

The Limpkin is a long-legged brown bird with white streaks and spots. It lives in swamps and along slow-moving streams in Florida. Its long, tweezer-like bill bends to the right so that it can eat one particular food item—the apple snail. When a snail is found, the Limpkin inserts its bill into the opening of the shell, snips the muscle attachment, and swallows the snail, without even breaking the shell!

PILEATED WOODPECKER

SCIENTIFIC NAME: *Dryocopus pileatus*
LENGTH: 16½ in (42 cm)
WINGSPAN: 29 in (74 cm)

If you see a huge, red-crested, black-and-white bird that makes your jaw drop in amazement, you are undoubtedly looking at a Pileated (PILL-ee-ay-ted) Woodpecker. The size of a crow, the Pileated is the biggest woodpecker in North America. A very loud drumming sound means the Pileated is drilling into a big tree or a fallen log in search of beetles and carpenter ants. Its call is a loud, piercing *kee-kee-kee.* Pileated Woodpeckers are most common in the dark, swampy forests of the Deep South, but also live throughout the eastern half of the U.S. and in the Pacific Northwest.

PROTHONOTARY WARBLER

SCIENTIFIC NAME: *Protonotaria citrea*
LENGTH: 5½ in (14 cm)
WINGSPAN: 8¾ in (22 cm)

A small bird with a very long name, the Prothonotary Warbler is a brilliant, golden-yellow spot of color in its dark, swampy home. The species got its name from the resemblance of its bright yellow plumage to the colorful robes worn by Vatican clerks (prothonotaries) who serve the pope. The Prothonotary is the only eastern wood-warbler that nests in tree cavities—often old holes carved out by Downy Woodpeckers —or even nesting boxes. Loss of habitat puts the Prothonotary Warbler at risk, both in its U.S. breeding grounds and in the Central and South American mangrove swamps where it spends the winter.

River
and **Marsh**

BLACK-CROWNED NIGHT-HERON

River and Marsh

HABITAT

SANDHILL CRANE

CANADA GOOSE

YELLOW WARBLER

RICH WITH WILDLIFE

Wherever you are, a river is probably not far away. Rivers can be huge watery highways, like the Mississippi or the Colorado, or they can be a summertime trickle that turns into a torrent in the spring. A marsh is a waterlogged area where grasses or reeds grow, but not many trees. Marshes are often found next to rivers and lakes. These freshwater areas are rich with wildlife of all kinds—from microscopic animals to predators such as Bald Eagles and river otters.

BALD EAGLE

DOUBLE-CRESTED CORMORANT

BELTED KINGFISHER

RED-WINGED BLACKBIRD

GREAT BLUE HERON

BLACK-CROWNED NIGHT-HERON

TREE SWALLOW

Great Blue Heron

THE LONG-LEGGED, MAJESTIC Great Blue Heron is the largest heron in North America, and can be found in wetland areas everywhere in the lower 48 states and much of Canada. The Great Blue is a patient hunter. It often stands motionless for long stretches of time waiting for a frog, fish, or snake to wander within range. Then, with lightning speed, its long neck propels its dagger-like bill toward the water to snatch up a meal. The catch is first subdued and then swallowed headfirst. Striding majestically through shallow water, or taking off with slow, powerful wing beats, its long legs trailing behind, the Great Blue Heron is an awe-inspiring sight. The heron's powerful wings measure six feet from tip to tip.

SCIENTIFIC NAME: *Ardea herodias*
LENGTH: 46 in (117 cm)
WINGSPAN: 72 in (183 cm)

VOICE

When arriving at their nest, Great Blues greet each other with a squawking *roh-roh-roh*. If the birds are disturbed, a clucking *go-go-go* builds to a loud *frawnk*, and the whole performance can last as long as 20 seconds. When threatened, Great Blues let loose with an ear-shattering *FRAWNK!* This call may be the reason some people know this bird as "Big Cranky."

FOOD

Great Blue Herons eat just about anything they can catch in or near the water, including fish, frogs, snakes, lizards, insects, and small mammals. They grab small prey in their strong bills and sometimes spear larger fish with the bill's daggerlike tip. Great Blues also hunt for rodents in grasslands and farm fields.

HABITAT & RANGE

Great Blue Herons live in both freshwater and saltwater environments. In the Northeast, they have benefited from an increase in the number of beavers. Beavers build dams across streams and along river edges that create ponds that are ideal hunting grounds. Their

TO KEEP its balance in flight, the Great Blue—like all herons—folds its neck into a compact **S-shape** and tucks it in close to its body while its long legs trail out behind.

A CLOSER LOOK

Pointed bill is used to grab prey, but usually not to stab it.

Breeding bird has ornate plumes on the head and hanging off the neck and back.

S-shaped neck is hinged in the middle to allow it to jab forward at its prey.

The color of its body is gray, even though its name says "blue."

Long, black legs allow wading in deep water where smaller herons can't go.

nesting areas are often located in swamps, on islands, or near lakes and ponds surrounded by forests. Great Blues that nest in Canada migrate south for the winter.

RANGE MAP KEY

- SUMMER (breeding)
- WINTER (nonbreeding)
- YEAR-ROUND

LOOKING GOOD

Not many people know the Great Blue's secret to good grooming: It carries a comb wherever it goes. The claw on the middle toe of each foot has special comblike teeth growing from it that are used for scratching and preening its handsome feathers. For an added touch, special feathers on it chest grow continually and produce "powder down" that is used to clean off swamp goo and fish slime.

Bald Eagle

THE BALD EAGLE became the United States' national emblem in 1782. This majestic bird's favorite food is fish, and flying low over the water, it will nab a large fish swimming near the surface in its talons or even wade into shallow water to grab one. In addition to being a fierce predator, it is also a thief and a scavenger. Rather than do its own fishing, it is more likely to attack an Osprey and steal its catch, or feed on dead fish or other carrion it finds on a riverbank. By the mid-1900s, Bald Eagles were seriously endangered because of hunting and pesticide pollution (DDT). Thanks to the efforts of conservationists, special protections were put in place. Today the Bald Eagle is thriving and can be found all across North America.

SCIENTIFIC NAME: *Haliaeetus leucocephalus*
LENGTH: 34 in (86 cm)
WINGSPAN: 80 in (203 cm)

VOICE

For such a large, powerful bird, the Bald Eagle has a surprisingly high-pitched voice and weak twittering call of *kwit kwit kee-kee-kee-kee-keer*.

FOOD

When they are available, fish are pretty much all that Bald Eagles eat. It takes time for an eagle to become an expert fish-catcher, so young birds are more likely to look for dead fish or try to steal a meal. When fish are scarce, eagles will hunt reptiles, turtles, frogs, shellfish, small mammals such as squirrels, and large birds like ducks or coots. Bald Eagles sometimes hunt together but are much more likely to steal food from each other than to share.

HABITAT & RANGE

Bald Eagles usually live near lakes, reservoirs, rivers, marshes, swamps, and seacoasts. They are also occasionally found in open, dry country or on mountaintops. In winter, large numbers of eagles gather to feed at garbage dumps, fish processing plants, near dams, and below hydroelectric plants, where fish are killed by passing through the water intakes.

IT TAKES about **five** years for a young Bald Eagle to reach adulthood and get a completely white head and tail.

A CLOSER LOOK

Only the adult has a white head and tail. Young eagles have brown heads and tails.

Huge yellow bill, hooked at the tip for tearing apart its prey

Heavy brown body

Large, very sharp talons for killing prey and carrying it off

Adult

They build huge nests of sticks, high up in a tree, often building on top of a previous year's nest. One nest in Ohio was used for 34 years and weighed more than two tons. Bald Eagles are most abundant in Alaska. In winter, many eagles gather along the Mississippi and Missouri Rivers.

RANGE MAP KEY

- SUMMER (breeding)
- MIGRATION
- WINTER (nonbreeding)
- YEAR-ROUND

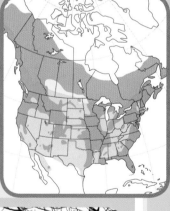

WINTERTIME IS VACATION TIME

During the winter months, eagles are likely to be found hanging out with other eagles in locations with lots of easy-to-obtain food. They don't really do much. A group of eagles studied in Washington State spent 98 percent of their time either perched or roosting (sleeping), and only 2 percent flying or feeding. By comparison, the spring and summer months are exhausting, with courtship, mating, nest-building, and hunting down enough food for a family of hungry, growing eaglets.

Belted Kingfisher

WHEN EXCITED OR FEELING threatened, the Belted Kingfisher raises its shaggy crest feathers, spreads its wings, and poses in ways that show off its large bill. Unlike many species of birds, the female kingfisher is more colorful than the male. True to its name, this bird is great at catching fish. Studying the water from an overhanging perch, the kingfisher spots its prey. Then, after a short flight or brief hover overhead, it dives headfirst into the water and grabs the fish with its bill. It then slams the fish against a branch to kill it, before swallowing it whole. Young birds are taught how to fish by their parents, who drop dead fish in the water for their young to practice on.

SCIENTIFIC NAME: *Megaceryle alcyon*
LENGTH: 13 in (33 cm)
WINGSPAN: 20 in (51 cm)

VITAL STATISTICS

VOICE

All kingfishers are members of the same family as the Laughing Kookaburra of Australia. Although not quite as loud as a kookaburra, these alert and highly territorial birds announce their presence to all comers with a loud, staccato rattle-call, heard year-round and often given in flight.

FOOD

Small fish, four to five inches long or less, make up most of the Belted Kingfisher's diet, which also includes crayfish, frogs, tadpoles, and insects. It hunts by hovering or from a perch overlooking clear waterways—it needs clear water in order to see its prey swimming below the surface. The parts of its prey that it can't digest—mostly scales and bones—get coughed up later as a pellet.

HABITAT & RANGE

Belted Kingfishers are found all across the country near rivers, streams, lakes, ponds, and estuaries with clear water and an abundance of fish. For nesting, they search for a nearby steep riverbank or gravel pit. There they dig a tunnel-like burrow that extends several feet or more into the bank. Birds that breed in the north migrate south in winter when rivers and lakes freeze over.

WHEN plunging headfirst into the water, the Belted Kingfisher sometimes submerges its **whole body** underwater.

A CLOSER LOOK

When a kingfisher is agitated its crest is held straight up.

Female *Male*

The male kingfisher has a single blue "belt" and the female has two, one blue and one rust-colored.

Tiny feet and short legs are good for perching and shuffling through the nest tunnel.

The large bill is used to grab a fish and also to subdue it.

RANGE MAP KEY

SUMMER (breeding)

WINTER (nonbreeding)

YEAR-ROUND

A WATERY KINGDOM

What matters most to a kingfisher is a good extent of clear water with lots of fish and a nearby dirt bank to dig a nest tunnel into. So, unlike most birds, a pair of kingfishers defends a stretch of water, not a plot of land. Their home territory is usually about a half mile of river or lakeshore from which all other kingfishers are chased off.

Red-winged Blackbird

THE RED-WINGED BLACKBIRD is one of the most abundant birds in North America. In early spring, males arrive back at their breeding marshes before the females and immediately start singing, flashing their vivid red shoulders, and claiming territory. The most aggressive, loudest, and flashiest male may attract up to 15 females. The females, which look a bit like streaky sparrows, take on most of the parenting duties. While the female is building a nest and later on incubating her eggs, the male Red-wing spends much of the day defending his territory from other males, nest predators (crows, hawks, snakes), and even people or livestock. Sometimes Red-wing males will band together to drive a large intruder away.

SCIENTIFIC NAME: *Agelaius phoeniceus*
LENGTH: 8¾ in (22 cm)
WINGSPAN: 13 in (33 cm)

VOICE

For many people, the male Red-winged Blackbird's liquid gurgling call—*konk-la-ree!* ending in a trill—is a signal that spring has begun, even if there is still snow on the ground and ice in the streams and marshes. Their most common call is a flat *chack*.

FOOD

In the summer, Red-wings eat a mixed diet of insects, seeds, and berries. During the winter, they eat seeds and grains, like corn and wheat, often feeding in huge flocks in farm fields. They will also visit bird feeders, where millet and corn are their favorite foods.

HABITAT & RANGE

Colonies of Red-winged Blackbirds nest in marshes, saltwater wetlands, riverside reed beds, roadside ditches, and suburban ponds if there are cattails growing at the edges. In winter, large numbers of Red-wings flock together and join up with other "black birds," such as grackles, cowbirds, and starlings. These winter flocks—sometimes with more than a million birds in them—gather in farm fields, livestock feedlots, marshes, and even in suburban neighborhoods. They begin to migrate as early as February and also live in Mexico and Central America.

RED-WINGED Blackbird nests are woven around an **upright** marsh plant and take females about **five** days to build.

A CLOSER LOOK

The female is brownish overall with streaks on the belly and a pale stripe over the eye.

Females

The male is glossy black with brilliant red and yellow shoulder patches (called "epaulets").

The sharply pointed bill is good for grabbing insects and seeds, and it can also be inserted into a likely spot and forcibly opened to expose hidden prey.

Male

RANGE MAP KEY

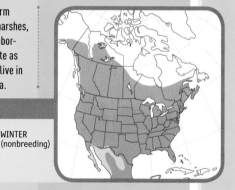

- ■ SUMMER (breeding)
- □ WINTER (nonbreeding)
- ■ YEAR-ROUND

THE RED BADGE OF COURAGE

Male Red-wings establish a breeding territory by singing and displaying the red epaulet feathers on their wings. These feathers can be raised, and when the shoulders are thrust outward, they blaze bright crimson in the sun; below the red is a line of yellow feathers. Higher perches make for a better show and are an indication of a male's dominance. If a weaker male is trespassing on another male's territory or wants to sneak through the marsh, he can hide his red shoulder patches to avoid being attacked by a more aggressive male.

Rivers are great places to see birds as they fly across open areas or feed along the shoreline. If you're planning a boating trip or just strolling by a river or marshland, see if you can spot these birds.

CANADA GOOSE

SCIENTIFIC NAME: *Branta canadensis*
LENGTH: 40 in (102 cm)
WINGSPAN: 55 in (140 cm)

Most people are familiar with the Canada Goose—brown body, long black neck, and white "chinstrap"—but did you know that during the past 50 years, many Canada Geese have stopped migrating to Canada? Large numbers have taken up year-round residence in city parks, reservoirs, riverbanks, ponds, airports, and golf courses all over North America. They graze on grass and a variety of pond and river plants. Their call is a nasal *honk-a-lonk* or two-syllable *ka-ronk*. Some Canada Geese still migrate in spring and fall.

DOUBLE-CRESTED CORMORANT

SCIENTIFIC NAME: *Phalacrocorax auritus*
LENGTH: 32 in (81 cm)
WINGSPAN: 52 in (132 cm)

This big, black, fish-eating bird is often seen perched on a riverbank or coastal pier with its wings held open to dry in the sun. Many waterbirds, such as ducks and geese, have waterproof feathers, but not the cormorant —its feathers can get soaked. This makes it easier for the cormorant to dive underwater and chase after fish, but it's not good for flying or staying warm. When the cormorant is swimming, sometimes all that is visible is its long, S-shaped neck and orange face. Cormorants nest in colonies and build big, bulky nests made of sticks.

TREE SWALLOW

SCIENTIFIC NAME: *Tachycineta bicolor*
LENGTH: 5¾ in (15 cm)
WINGSPAN: 14½ in (37 cm)

Tree Swallows are common around marshes and open fields. These steely blue and white birds are often seen flying over rivers, ponds, and fields as they chase down flying insects. Most Tree Swallows nest in old woodpecker holes or in birdhouses provided by people. In the winter months and during migration, Tree Swallows gather in marshy areas in flocks of thousands of birds, where they roost together during the night. When flying insects are unavailable, Tree Swallows can survive on a diet of berries. This ability allows them to linger in fall and to spend the winter farther north than any other swallow.

SANDHILL CRANE

SCIENTIFIC NAME: *Grus canadensis*
LENGTH: 46 in (117 cm)
WINGSPAN: 77 in (196 cm)

The Sandhill Crane is a big gray bird that can be mistaken for a Great Blue Heron (see pp. 104–105). Cranes nest in freshwater marshes in the Northwest, upper Great Lakes, and Canada, and spend the winter months farther south, from California to Florida. There are only 15 species of cranes in the world and most of them are endangered. The Sandhill Crane is one of the few that is doing well. In early spring, about half a million cranes gather along the Platte River in Nebraska before flying north to their breeding areas.

BLACK-CROWNED NIGHT-HERON

SCIENTIFIC NAME: *Nycticorax nycticorax*
LENGTH: 25 in (64 cm)
WINGSPAN: 44 in (112 cm)

If their nesting colony is disturbed, the young Black-crowned Night-Herons will poop and puke on the intruder. Their strategy must work—the Black-crowned is the most widely distributed heron in the world. Nesting colonies are located in trees near marshes, riversides, and swamps across the U.S. The adult is a short-legged heron with a gray body and black cap and back; young birds are brown and spotted with white. True to its name, the Black-crowned Night-Heron feeds mainly at dusk and during the night.

YELLOW WARBLER

SCIENTIFIC NAME: *Setophaga petechia*
LENGTH: 5 in (13 cm)
WINGSPAN: 8 in (20 cm)

The bright, butter-colored Yellow Warbler is a small songbird that nests in North America and migrates to Central and South America for the winter. For some, this includes a nonstop flight across the Gulf of Mexico, a feat of amazing endurance given its tiny size. In summer, Yellow Warblers nest in willows and thickets alongside rivers, streams, and marshes across much of the United States and Canada and eat insects, such as caterpillars, midges, and leafhoppers. Sometimes a female Brown-headed Cowbird will sneak into a warbler's nest and lay her own eggs there.

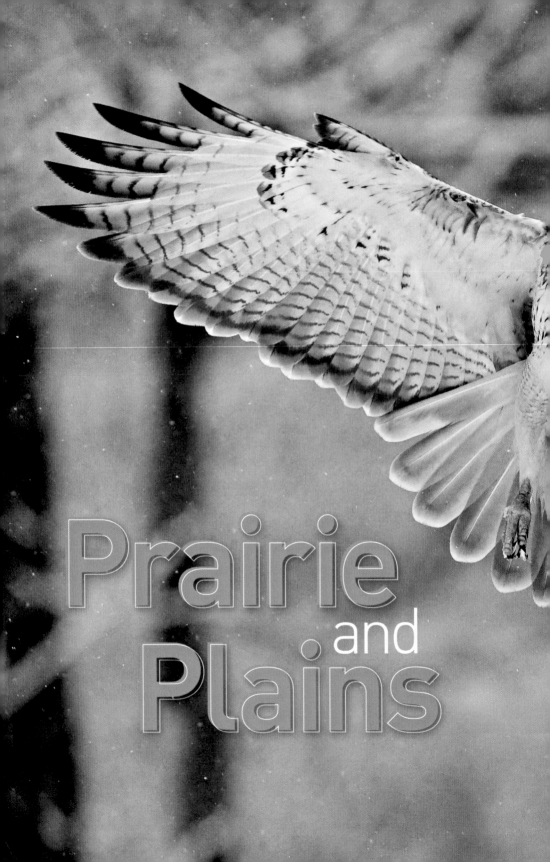

Prairie
and
Plains

RED-TAILED HAWK

Prairie and Plains

HABITAT

SCISSOR-TAILED FLYCATCHER

PRAIRIE FALCON

BURROWING OWL

HOME ON THE RANGE

The great midsection of the United States was once a vast rolling sea of wild grass with an abundance of animals and birds. Huge herds of buffalo migrated across the prairie, which they shared with abundant deer, elk, and antelope. Today, most of the once wild prairie has been converted to farmland and the remaining buffalo are mostly found in national parks. Millions of wild birds, however, still migrate across the region, nest and breed there in the summer, or live there year-round.

WESTERN KINGBIRD

RED-TAILED HAWK

WESTERN MEADOWLARK

BLACK-BILLED MAGPIE

HORNED LARK

SHARP-TAILED GROUSE

DICKCISSEL

Red-tailed Hawk

THE RED-TAILED HAWK—the most common hawk in North America, with a global population of about two million birds—is also one of the easiest to see. Driving through open country, you'll probably see this bulky, broad-winged hawk soaring over fields, showing its rusty red tail feathers. It perches in the open and is often seen sitting atop roadside utility poles or fence posts. Red-tails build their nests at the top of tall trees, saguaro cacti, power line towers, or on a cliff ledge. In 1992 a male Red-tailed Hawk, known to his fans as "Pale Male," began nesting with his mate on the stone ledge of an apartment building in New York City. He has nested in the same area for more than 20 years (wild Red-tails can live for more than 30 years).

SCIENTIFIC NAME: *Buteo jamaicensis*
LENGTH: 22 in (56 cm)
WINGSPAN: 50 in (127 cm)

VITAL STATISTICS

VOICE

Red-tailed Hawks have a distinctive call, especially when they are flying—a harsh, descending *keee-eerrrrrr*. Their call can often be heard in the background of a film or television show set in the Old West.

FOOD

Red-tailed Hawks often hunt by sitting on a perch high up that allows them to survey the area below. They also hunt by cruising over open areas or soaring high in the air. Favorite prey includes small mammals such as mice, moles, rabbits, and voles. In the West, they seek out ground squirrels and jackrabbits. They also eat reptiles and larger birds. Most prey is captured and killed on the ground, then carried to a feeding perch to be eaten.

HABITAT & RANGE

Red-tailed Hawks live in various habitats, from mountains and woodlands to prairies and deserts, as well as city and suburban areas that have trees and open space. The Great Plains is a great place to see them soaring over the prairie.

JUVENILES have brown tails with numerous dark **bars** and are more streaked underneath.

A CLOSER LOOK

Juvenile

Adult

Hooked bill is used for tearing apart its prey.

Large, dark eyes can spot small animals from great distances. Juveniles have yellow eyes.

Long, broad wings are perfect for soaring high in the sky.

The "red" tail of the adult is really more of a rusty brown color.

In fall, most of the Red-tails that nested in Canada migrate to the United States. In many places, they are year-round residents.

RANGE MAP KEY

SUMMER (breeding)

WINTER (nonbreeding)

YEAR-ROUND

SKY-DANCING

Courting Red-tails have some great aerial dance moves that help them bond with each other. Typically, both birds start off by soaring in wide circles at high altitudes and then the male starts showing off. Upon gaining altitude, he dives steeply, pulls out of the dive, and shoots upward. After repeating this several times, he approaches the female from above and extends his legs to touch her, then the birds may grasp one another's beaks or interlock talons and spiral toward the ground. Sometimes these aerial acrobatics include courtship feeding, with the male passing food to the female. And, of course, the whole affair is accompanied by piercing screams from both parties.

Western Kingbird

THE WESTERN KINGBIRD is a summer bird over most of the Great Plains and the western states. "Here I am! Look at me!" the handsome kingbird seems to be saying as it sits on a prominent perch, for all to see. Often found where people live, they may perch low on a fence post or barbed wire or higher up on utility wires. A curious courtship display is called the "Tumble Flight," during which the male flies to a height of about 50 feet, then turns sharply and begins a tumbling descent full of twists and flips accompanied with loud vocalizations. For its nest, the kingbird builds a bulky construction of twigs, bark, and rootlets, which is lined with various soft fibers.

SCIENTIFIC NAME: *Tyrannus verticalis*
LENGTH: 8¾ in (22 cm)
WINGSPAN: 15½ in (39 cm)

VOICE

The Western Kingbird's song is a fast, squeaky *pik pik peek PEEK-a-loo*. The common call is a sharp *kip*, given singly or in a stuttering series.

FOOD

Western Kingbirds feed on insects. Most prey is captured during flights from a perch (called "sallies"). Aerial pursuits sometimes take twisting, acrobatic turns as the bird follows a flying insect. Kingbirds also catch insects on the ground or pluck them off bushes. Late in the summer and in the fall, they add fruit to their diet.

HABITAT & RANGE

Western Kingbirds are summer residents from the Great Plains and west to California. They prefer dry country interspersed with trees—grasslands, foothills, farmland, and ranchland, as well as towns and urban parks. They construct their nests on the outer branches of a tree or shrub or on man-made structures such as a building, a utility pole, or even a city lamppost or backyard

THE WESTERN Kingbird's bill can catch large **insects,** such as grasshoppers and dragonflies.

A CLOSER LOOK

Adult's red-orange crown is kept hidden, unless the bird gets really irritated.

Pale tones and earthy colors of its feathers blend in with the colors of the prairie.

Yellow belly and blackish tail with white edges

Kingbirds (and all flycatchers) have tiny feet that are useful only for perching on small branches, wires, or posts.

basketball hoop, braced against the backboard. They spend winters mainly in Mexico and Central America, and a few birds wander to the East Coast every fall.

RANGE MAP KEY

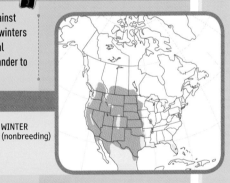

- ▢ SUMMER (breeding)
- ▢ WINTER (nonbreeding)
- ▢ MIGRATION

KING OF THE PRAIRIE

The Western Kingbird likes a perch with a good view. Any insect that flies by is easily picked off, but that's not the only reason. This kingbird is also on the lookout for trespassers—no matter how big. Any hawk, eagle, crow, or raven that gets too near its nest tree is relentlessly chased and pecked. Sometimes the kingbird even lands on the bigger bird's back! Being such an agile flier, the kingbird is in little danger of getting caught and it isn't long before the intruder changes course, glad to be rid of the fearless smaller bird with a big attitude.

Black-billed Magpie

THE INQUISITIVE Black-billed Magpie is easy to spot in many open spaces in the West because of its showy black-and-white plumage and extremely long tail. Magpies, in the same family as crows and jays, exhibit many fascinating behaviors. They'll follow a coyote to steal its food—one bird sneaks up behind the coyote and pulls its tail, and when it turns toward the offending bird, another magpie in the group steals the food. They also conduct "funerals" where birds will gather in a noisy flock around a dead magpie for 10 to 15 minutes and then all fly off in silence. Magpies hop and walk on the ground with a confident swagger and fly with steady, rowing wing beats often ending with a swooping glide to a perch.

SCIENTIFIC NAME: *Pica hudsonia*
LENGTH: 19 in (48 cm)
WINGSPAN: 25 in (64 cm)

VITAL STATISTICS

VOICE

Magpies have a variety of different calls including a quick series of *mag, mag, mag* and a whining, rising *mee-aaah*.

FOOD

Magpies are omnivores. They eat animal matter, either from scavenged carrion and human garbage or from animals they catch and kill—rodents, reptiles, insects, ticks (picked off live deer and moose), newly hatched baby birds, or bird eggs. They also eat large amounts of grain and fruit. They forage on the ground, rarely in trees. Magpies often hide stashes of excess food in different locations.

HABITAT & RANGE

The Black-billed Magpie is a year-round resident of prairies, scrublands, and rangelands, often near a stream, lake, or pond. Magpies are also at home in suburbs, towns, and urban parks. A magpie's nest in a tree or tall shrub is often quite noticeable—a bulky, ball-shaped construction of sticks that has an inside cup lined with mud, dung, and animal hair.

IN FLIGHT, the flashing **white** wing patches and two racing stripes on the back are hard to miss.

A CLOSER LOOK

From a distance a magpie looks black and white, but close up the black feathers glitter with blue, green and purple colors, especially on the wings and tail.

White wing tips are hidden when the bird is perched but are flashed during aggressive displays.

Strong bill is capable of catching and killing small animals, such as rodents.

Magpies walk on the ground and have strong legs and feet.

The tail is almost as long as the body and allows it to make quick changes in flight direction. Males with longer tails are preferred by females.

Magpies don't migrate, even the ones that live as far north as Alaska.

RANGE MAP KEY

YEAR-ROUND

WHAT'S YOURS IS MINE

Magpies don't have much use for property rights. Long before Columbus visited the New World, magpies were following bison-hunting Native Americans and living on the leftovers of their hunts. When the Lewis and Clark expedition first encountered magpies in 1804 in South Dakota, the birds showed no fear of man and boldly entered their tents to steal meat.

Western Meadowlark

THE YELLOW-BREASTED Western Meadowlark is a colorful member of the blackbird family. The male sings his cheerful song all across the western United States. However, what to our ears is sweet music is serious business to the meadowlark—his song tells other meadowlarks to keep away.

SCIENTIFIC NAME: *Sturnella neglecta*
LENGTH: 9½ in (24 cm)
WINGSPAN: 14½ in (37 cm)

Any trespassing males are vigorously chased until they leave the area. If an intruder resists, he may be attacked. In the Great Plains and upper Midwest, the Western Meadowlark's range overlaps that of the closely related Eastern Meadowlark. Even though the two species look very similar, they sing different songs and don't interbreed. Meriwether Lewis was the first to point out the subtle differences between the meadowlarks in 1805.

VOICE

The male Western Meadowlark usually sings his song from a prominent perch like a fence post or the top of an isolated bush. The loud, bubbly song is a burst of flute-like whistles, *tuuu-weet-too-TWLEEDLOoo.*

FOOD

During the summer, meadowlarks eat insects, especially grasshoppers and crickets. In fall and winter, when there are few insects to be found, their diet is mostly weed seeds and grain.

HABITAT & RANGE

The Western Meadowlark inhabits dry rangelands, native grasslands, roadsides, large pastures, desert grasslands, and, in winter, other open areas such as croplands, feedlots, and large lawns. The female builds her nest on the ground in tall grass. The nest is a cup of grass with a domed roof woven into the grass around it. The entrance to this snug little home is a tunnel located on one side. Some birds migrate south, but birds can survive cold winters if the ground isn't

THE yellow breast and black V are more than pretty decoration; males with the brightest colors are preferred by females and **control** the best territories.

A CLOSER LOOK

Uses its sharply pointed bill to probe into the ground for insects.

The brown and tan stripes on the upperparts are good camouflage, protecting birds from being spotted by a hawk flying overhead.

Adult

White outer tail feathers are hidden except when the bird flies or twitches its tail.

Juvenile

completely snow-covered. Western Meadowlarks also live in Mexico.

RANGE MAP KEY

SUMMER (breeding)	WINTER (nonbreeding)
MIGRATION	YEAR-ROUND

MIRROR, MIRROR ON THE WALL ...

If "state bird" status is a type of popularity contest in the bird world, only the Northern Cardinal tops the Western Meadowlark. The Northern Cardinal is the state bird of seven states: Illinois, Indiana, Kentucky, North Carolina, Ohio, Virginia, and West Virginia. Close behind, the Western Meadowlark is the state bird of six states: Kansas, Montana, Nebraska, North Dakota, Oregon, and Wyoming.

Some birds don't like trees. Such species feel more at home flying in wide-open spaces or perching on the ground. Here are six more of these prairie and plains birds you can look for.

SHARP-TAILED GROUSE

SCIENTIFIC NAME: *Tympanuchus phasianellus*
LENGTH: 17 in (43 cm)
WINGSPAN: 25 in (64 cm)

The chicken-sized Sharp-tailed Grouse is a ground-loving bird that lives in prairie grasslands with scattered trees and also in farm fields where they eat—seeds, leaves, roots, wild fruits and nuts, and insects. This bird was an important source of food for Native Americans and the early settlers of the Great Plains and western Canada. Its name refers to the pointed tail feathers that are held high when the male does his courtship dance. Males gather on traditional dancing grounds called "leks" where they strut, bow, and do a foot-stomping stutter dance to impress females.

PRAIRIE FALCON

SCIENTIFIC NAME: *Falco mexicanus*
LENGTH: 16 in (41 cm)
WINGSPAN: 40 in (102 cm)

The Prairie Falcon hunts its prey from the sky over dry western plains, prairies, and deserts. Its quarry is varied—some falcons specialize in ground squirrels, whereas others attack larger birds like Sharp-tailed Grouse (see left). Falcons also hunt jackrabbits, small birds, lizards, and large insects. The falcon's long wings and strong muscles make it very fast in the air, and after it spots a victim it simply chases it down, grabs it with its talons, and quickly dispatches it with a bite to the neck. Prairie Falcons usually choose a cliff ledge protected by an overhanging rock for nesting and sometimes share the mountainside with a pair of Common Ravens or Golden Eagles.

BURROWING OWL

SCIENTIFIC NAME: *Athene cunicularia*
LENGTH: 9½ in (24 cm)
WINGSPAN: 21 in (53 cm)

These diminutive, somewhat comical-looking owls nest in holes in the ground in open, scrubby terrain, grasslands, golf courses, and airports. They rarely dig their own holes; instead, they take over an unused burrow of a rabbit, skunk, armadillo, or prairie dog. During the day, though well camouflaged, they can be seen sitting near the entrance to their burrow. They hunt for insects by day and small mammals at night. In the Southwest, Burrowing Owls are year-round residents; those that nest farther north migrate south in the fall. The destruction of prairie dog towns and agricultural growth have greatly decreased this owl's numbers.

SCISSOR-TAILED FLYCATCHER

SCIENTIFIC NAME: *Tyrannus forficatus*
LENGTH: 13 in (33 cm)
WINGSPAN: 15 in (38 cm)

Oklahoma's state bird was well chosen— the Scissor-tail's small breeding range is centered directly on that state. From spring through fall it's hard to miss this extraordinary bird that sits conspicuously on roadside fences and low shrubs, tail held tightly closed and looking like a long stick. When pursuing flying insects, the surprising tail flares open, revealing its scissorlike shape and also the bird's beautiful salmon pink belly. The summer home of the so-called Texas Bird-of-Paradise is also the center of the tornado belt. Scissor-tails migrate to Mexico and Central America for the winter months.

HORNED LARK

SCIENTIFIC NAME: *Eremophila alpestris*
LENGTH: 7 in (18 cm)
WINGSPAN: 12 in (30 cm)

The grasslands and prairies of North America have a large population of Horned Larks, but this ground-loving species also lives in Europe, North Africa, and central Asia. Regardless of where they live, they prefer barren country, dry prairies, deserts, and agricultural lands. Larks that nest on the Arctic tundra join prairie-nesting birds and form large flocks in the winter months. All Horned Larks have a black mask and bib with two black "horns" (feather tufts) growing from the top of the head. Adults eat weed and grass seeds, but they feed their young a more protein-rich diet of insects. The Horned Lark's song is a series of high-pitched, tinkling notes.

DICKCISSEL

SCIENTIFIC NAME: *Spiza americana*
LENGTH: 6¼ in (16 cm)
WINGSPAN: 9¾ in (25 cm)

Like the chickadee and the phoebe, the name Dickcissel (DIK-sis-sul) comes from the song it sings: *dick dick dick ciss ciss cissel*. About the size of a large sparrow, the Dickcissel is a very common breeding bird in grasslands, prairies, and hayfields throughout the central United States. With its yellow breast and the black bib of the male, it resembles a miniature meadowlark (see pp. 124–125), which it often has for a neighbor. Dickcissels eat seeds and insects and build their nests near the ground, hidden by tall grass. In the fall, birds migrate to Central and South America.

CACTUS WREN

Deserts

Deserts

HABITAT

HARRIS'S HAWK

WHITE-WINGED DOVE

GAMBEL'S QUAIL

SURPRISINGLY FULL OF LIFE

Most deserts, including those of the American Southwest, are not wastelands of endless sand dunes. The Sonoran Desert stretching from California to Arizona is full of cacti, shrubs, and even a few rivers. Birds and other animals that are adapted to the heat and dryness do more than survive there—they thrive.

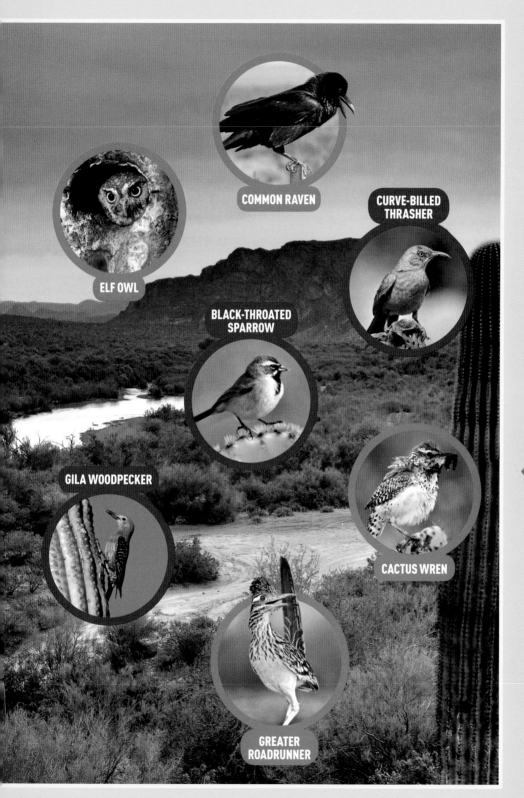

COMMON RAVEN

CURVE-BILLED THRASHER

ELF OWL

BLACK-THROATED SPARROW

GILA WOODPECKER

CACTUS WREN

GREATER ROADRUNNER

Harris's Hawk

THESE REMARKABLE raptors are best known for forming avian "wolf packs," family groups that hunt together, with each bird having a specific job. Some spread out and conceal themselves on perches, waiting patiently, while others find and flush a ground squirrel or speedy jackrabbit out into the open. When this happens, a "lookout" bird calls loudly and the fleeing prey runs right into the waiting talons of one of the hunters. The desert-dwelling Harris's Hawk is easy to identify. It has a dark brown body with beautiful chestnut inner wings and leg feathers. In flight its long black tail with a white base and a white tip is hard to miss. If you're in cactus country and you see a Harris's Hawk, look around, as there are probably more nearby.

SCIENTIFIC NAME: *Parabuteo unicinctus*
LENGTH: 21 in (53 cm)
WINGSPAN: 46 in (117 cm)

VOICE

The Harris's Hawk has a high-pitched voice. Its calls are a series of harsh *eeeeer eeeeer eeeeer* cries.

FOOD

The Harris's Hawk's favorite prey are small to medium-size mammals like kangaroo rats, wood rats, ground squirrels, and jackrabbits; they also attack medium-size birds like quail and woodpeckers, and they eat lizards and large insects when they are abundant.

HABITAT & RANGE

Harris's Hawks like it hot. They are found mostly in saguaro cactus desert in Arizona and mesquite brush country in Texas and New Mexico. Rivers lined with cottonwoods and other types of trees and brush are also wild places where they can be found. Recently, more and more Harris's Hawks have taken up residence in the suburbs of some cities in the desert Southwest, such as Phoenix and Tucson, Arizona. Harris's Hawks are permanent residents—they do not migrate. These birds also live in Central and South America, as far south as southern Chile.

HARRIS'S Hawks often build their stick nests nestled in the arms of a large saguaro **cactus** or at the top of a tree.

A CLOSER LOOK

Long legs are useful for grabbing prey and these hawks can run and hop surprisingly fast when chasing after a meal.

Long black tail with white tip and base; a long tail helps when making very sharp turns.

Skin on the face, legs, and toes is bright yellow.

Long black talons are used for catching prey.

RANGE MAP KEY

YEAR-ROUND

A PLACE FOR EVERYONE

Within a group of Harris's Hawks, each bird has a place in the "pecking order" and rarely challenges a bird of a higher rank. The most dominant bird is the "alpha" breeding female, followed by the "alpha" breeding male. Of lesser rank are the "beta" male helpers, followed by one to four "gamma" helpers at the bottom. "Gammas" are usually younger birds.

Greater Roadrunner

THE AMAZING Greater Roadrunner—the state bird of New Mexico—is a ground-dwelling member of the cuckoo family that flies only when absolutely necessary. They may not fly much, but Greater Roadrunners run at speeds up to 18 miles an hour when chasing prey or escaping a predator.

SCIENTIFIC NAME: *Geococcyx californianus*
LENGTH: 23 in (58 cm)
WINGSPAN: 22 in (56 cm)

They are also well adapted to living in their desert environment. Although they will drink water if it is available, roadrunners can survive without drinking if they are able to consume prey with high enough moisture content. Without water, they have a lot of extra salt in their bodies, but they've solved that problem. Roadrunners have a small gland in the corner of each eye that helps to eliminate extra salt.

VOICE

The roadrunner's primary call is a dove-like, loud *coo-coo-coo-coo* trailing off at the end. Also a sharp, loud *chuk-chuk-chuk-chuk!*

FOOD

The roadrunner's diet includes small mammals like mice and young ground squirrels, birds, insects, spiders, lizards, and snakes. Tarantulas, scorpions, centipedes, and rattlesnakes are all on the menu. Large food items are beaten repeatedly against the ground to soften them up before swallowing, and roadrunners seem to suffer no ill effects from eating venomous prey.

HABITAT & RANGE

Roadrunners live in open desert areas with some brush, like the Sonoran Desert. They can also be found in areas of Texas. Although the male helps to collect twigs to build a nest, the female actually constructs it, hiding it in a low bush or cactus. And sometimes they really do run on roads—dirt roads through the desert are good pathways through the cactus and thorny brush. Roadrunners live in the same place year-round. They are also found in Mexico.

WHEN RUNNING, the roadrunner often uses its wings and tail as rudders to **steer** with.

A CLOSER LOOK

Shiny black crest is raised when the roadrunner is on alert or agitated.

The heavy bill is long and slightly hooked at the tip.

Tail is very long and is tipped with white.

Wings are short; roadrunners don't fly very much.

Large feet and long legs for running through the desert

RANGE MAP KEY

☐ YEAR-ROUND

STRONG MAGIC

The Hopi, and other Pueblo tribes of the Southwest, revered the roadrunner and told stories of its bravery and endurance. Roadrunners were medicine birds, and drawings of the roadrunner's X-shaped footprints were sacred symbols that could ward off evil. The footprints offered protection because they looked the same coming and going—the roadrunner's foot has two toes facing forward and two facing backward, an unusual arrangement in birds. Any dangerous spirits that were trying to follow you wouldn't know which way to go.

Elf Owl

THE ELF OWL is the tiniest owl in the world—about the size of a sparrow—and looks like a toy soldier next to its big cousin the Great Horned Owl (see pp. 62–63). Even so, these tiny desert predators have all the standard owl equipment: sharp talons, hooked beak, silent wings, nighttime vision, and sharp hearing. But, rather than hunting rats and squirrels, these owls do battle with moths and beetles every night. Elf Owls nest in an old woodpecker hole carved into a tree or saguaro cactus. Nesting in a hole helps shelter them from the hot sun, and a pair of owls may use the same nest hole for a number of years. Nest holes are valuable real estate and are vigorously defended from other hole-nesting birds.

SCIENTIFIC NAME: *Micrathene whitneyi*

LENGTH: 5¼ in (13 cm)

WINGSPAN: 13 in (33 cm)

VOICE

Despite their small size, Elf Owls sing very loud chattering songs. The sound—different from all other North American owls—has been compared to the high-pitched yipping of a puppy.

FOOD

Elf Owls eat large insects, like moths, crickets, and beetles; occasionally they'll consume scorpions, spiders, and small lizards. They usually hunt from a perch and fly out after spotting a target, but they also land on the ground and pursue prey on foot for short distances. The insect parts that Elf Owls cannot digest are coughed up in compact pellets after a few hours.

HABITAT & RANGE

In the United States, Elf Owls live in southern Arizona, southern New Mexico, and western Texas. Although they are fairly common in lowland desert areas with saguaro cactus and thorny woodlands, they also live at higher elevations in streamside forests and mountain

INSIDE a saguaro cactus, a pair of Elf Owls will raise a family of two to four tiny **owlets.** The young owls leave the nest hole as soon as they can **fly.**

A CLOSER LOOK

Large yellow eyes gather in lots of light and face forward (like your eyes) for judging distance to a target.

Large rounded head with no ear tufts

The hooked bill and large mouth is mostly hidden by feathers.

Plumage is a combination of reddish brown, gray, and white.

Big feet, for such a small bird, armed with razor sharp talons

Wing feathers have soft edges so a flying owl makes no sound when hunting.

canyons. Sometimes migrating birds get lost, and Elf Owls have been found on oil platforms in the middle of the Gulf of Mexico. In the winter, Elf Owls live in Mexico.

RANGE MAP KEY

SUMMER (breeding)

WINTER (nonbreeding)

MIGRATION

YEAR-ROUND

ALWAYS FULL

Elf Owls are effective hunters, often catching more than they or their owlets can eat right away. The parent owls select the largest food items—sphinx moths, scorpions (with stingers removed), large beetles—and store them right in the nest with the owlets. Who knows when the craving for a juicy moth or crunchy scorpion will hit?

Cactus Wren

THE CACTUS WREN—the largest wren in North America and the state bird of Arizona—is well suited for life in the cactus-filled deserts of the Southwest. It is able to survive without a source of water, obtaining all the fluid it needs from the insects it eats or a bite of juicy cactus fruit. Pairs stay together all year and are often seen as they feed and call to each other. In late summer, entire families can be seen hopping on the ground, posturing with spread wings and tails, and generally being noisy. They often use their long bills to move fallen leaves or flip over a small rock to look for a tasty insect. Cactus Wrens also live around people in desert suburbs, especially in yards landscaped with cacti.

SCIENTIFIC NAME: *Campylorhynchus brunneicapillus*
LENGTH: 8½ in (22 cm)
WINGSPAN: 11 in (28 cm)

VOICE

Harsh and low pitched, the Cactus Wren's rapid song, *char char char char char char char*, increases in volume from beginning to end—it sounds like someone trying and failing to start an old car. All year long, even in the middle of the day when most desert birds are quiet, the wrens keep singing.

FOOD

Cactus Wrens eat insects and spiders. Their favorite foods are beetles, ants, wasps, grasshoppers, butterflies, and moths. Always on the lookout for a new food source, suburban-dwelling Cactus Wrens have discovered how to pick smashed bugs from the front grilles of parked cars.

HABITAT & RANGE

Cactus Wrens build their nests, perch, and hunt for prey amid the sharp spines of desert vegetation, most often cholla and saguaro cacti. They are also found in mesquite brush, among yucca plants, and in towns and coastal areas where cactus and thorny shrubs grows. Cactus Wrens do not migrate, and they may hatch and raise as many as three families in a single year. They also live in Mexico.

WITH the bottoms of its toes protected by tough **leathery** skin, the Cactus Wren can perch anywhere it wants to.

A CLOSER LOOK

Bill is an all-purpose tool, large enough to deal with a big caterpillar and delicate enough to pick up a tiny ant.

White stripe over the eye

Spots on the breast are variable; some birds have lots.

Streaks and bars on the back and wings are good camouflage.

Fairly long legs and strong feet for walking on the desert floor or perching on thorny plants

Tail is long and crossed with black bands.

RANGE MAP KEY

YEAR-ROUND

MASTER BUILDER

Nest building is an important skill that all Cactus Wrens must learn. The complicated nest—usually nestled in the arms of a cholla cactus or other spiny plant—is a large, ball-shaped construction of sticks and weed stems. It has a central chamber lined with feathers and is connected to the outside by a short tunnel, with a convenient "doorstep" perch at the front of the tunnel. Each pair builds several bulky nests in their territory and uses them for roosting year-round. Young birds start building their own nests for nighttime roosting when about four months old.

Mini-Profiles

DESERTS

GAMBEL'S QUAIL

SCIENTIFIC NAME: *Callipepla gambelii*
LENGTH: 11 in (28 cm)
WINGSPAN: 15 in (38 cm)

The Gambel's Quail is a plump, short-tailed bird of the desert Southwest with a loud, easy-to-remember call, *chi-CA-go-go*. Males and females both have a curious, comma-shaped topknot of feathers that bobs forward. Because they are tame and sociable, Gambel's have adapted well to the increasing number of people living in desert areas. They frequently come to backyards for birdseed and an essential drink of water. Out in the desert, family groups—coveys—scour the ground for seeds and insects, and often add buds, small cactus fruits, and berries to their diet.

WHITE-WINGED DOVE

SCIENTIFIC NAME: *Zenaida asiatica*
LENGTH: 11½ in (29 cm)
WINGSPAN: 19 in (48 cm)

Some desert birds are easy to see as they soar overhead, but many others stay hidden among the cacti and rocks. Lots of birds call the desert home. Here are six more of them you can watch for.

The White-winged Dove is a common summer sight near the Mexican border, and its drawn-out hooting call—"who-cooks-for-you" —is heard throughout the day. When it flies, a large white wing patch is visible, but, when the wing is folded, only a thin white stripe is left in view. And check out this bird's amazing orange eyes surrounded by powder blue skin—it looks like it's wearing makeup. Seeds and fruits make up its natural diet, but it also is attracted to bird feeders. White-winged Doves nest in trees and cacti, often in small colonies.

GILA WOODPECKER

SCIENTIFIC NAME: *Melanerpes uropygialis*
LENGTH: 9 in (24 cm)
WINGSPAN: 16 in (41 cm)

The zebra-striped back of the Gila Woodpecker is very noticeable as it clings to the side of a tall saguaro cactus. The tan head of the male is topped with a cap of red feathers that is absent in the female. They eat insects, supplemented with cactus fruit and mistletoe berries, and have learned how to hang onto a hummingbird feeder and lick up the sugary water. Many desert residents owe their cozy cavity homes to these industrious woodpeckers. Excavating a nest hole is a big project and both members of a woodpecker pair work on it. After all the excavating is done, the cavity has to dry out and the birds must wait for several months until the cactus grows an inner casing of fiber around the cavity—like a scab.

COMMON RAVEN

SCIENTIFIC NAME: *Corvus corax*
LENGTH: 24 in (61 cm)
WINGSPAN: 53 in (135 cm)

One of the most intelligent birds, the Common Raven is completely black, but it's much larger than a crow and also has a heavier bill and shaggy neck feathers. With long wings and a wedge-shaped tail, the raven can soar with ease and even plays games in the air, such as dropping and catching a stick or flying upside down. Ravens live in many different places, from deserts to high mountains to northern forests. Ravens eat just about anything: scavenged carrion, human garbage, small animals, large insects, baby birds, fish, and even wolf dung.

CURVE-BILLED THRASHER

SCIENTIFIC NAME: *Toxostoma curvirostre*
LENGTH: 11 in (28 cm)
WINGSPAN: 13½ in (34 cm)

The Curve-billed Thrasher is a common year-round resident found from the cactus-rich Sonoran Desert of Arizona to the brushlands of West Texas. It can be spotted calling loudly from atop a saguaro or prickly pear cactus, or even a street sign! The calls are very distinctive: a loud *whit-wheet* (in Arizona) or *whit-whit* (in Texas). If you live in a suburban desert community, this thrasher may be living in your backyard. Look for a brownish bird with a thick curved bill, long tail, and orange eyes. Eating a wide variety of insect prey, its diet is supplemented with seeds, wild berries, and cactus fruit.

BLACK-THROATED SPARROW

SCIENTIFIC NAME: *Amphispiza bilineata*
LENGTH: 5½ in (14 cm)
WINGSPAN: 7¾ in (20 cm)

The Black-throated Sparrow is a common desert bird but also somewhat of a mystery. Few ornithologists (bird scientists) have studied the Black-throated Sparrow as much as they have other sparrows, so there is much to be discovered about its habits and behavior. Bird-watchers enjoy seeing them because they are handsome and easy to identify. The large black bib and bold white face stripes give the adult a dressed-up look, but young birds are plainer and have brown streaks instead of a black bib. The Black-throated Sparrow lives in the desert Southwest and as far north as southern Idaho and west into California.

Western
Mountains

GOLDEN EAGLE

Western Mountains

HABITAT

WHITE-THROATED SWIFT

STELLER'S JAY

WESTERN TANAGER

ROCKY MOUNTAIN ADVENTURE

The Rockies are a mighty spine of tall mountains that run from Canada all the way south to Mexico, dividing the Great Plains from the western states and forming the Continental Divide. Many of the highest areas are protected as public parks and forests of breathtaking beauty, where families can experience the grandeur of nature and have fun going camping, hiking, and river rafting. The Rockies are a terrific place to see wildlife, and there are lots of special birds to find on a Rocky Mountain adventure.

GOLDEN EAGLE

VIOLET-GREEN SWALLOW

MOUNTAIN BLUEBIRD

CLARK'S NUTCRACKER

BROAD-TAILED HUMMINGBIRD

WHITE-TAILED PTARMIGAN

AMERICAN DIPPER

145

Golden Eagle

THE GOLDEN EAGLE, named for the golden feathers on its head and neck, is one of the largest and fiercest hunters in the North American bird world. The huge raptor—it has a seven-foot wingspan—can soar effortlessly on rising air currents and spot a prey animal far below using its "eagle-eyed" vision. With a dive that can reach 200 miles an hour, any rabbit or ground squirrel doesn't stand a chance. Native Americans regarded the eagle as a sacred bird with special powers. Because the Golden Eagle's feathers play an important role in the religious ceremonies of the Hopi nation, they have been given special permission from the United States government to remove hatched eagles from their nests and raise them in captivity.

SCIENTIFIC NAME: *Aquila chrysaetos*
LENGTH: 35 in (89 cm)
WINGSPAN: 84 in (213 cm)

VOICE

Golden Eagles are not very vocal. Their call is a high, weak whistle most often heard during nesting season.

FOOD

Favorite foods are small mammals—mice and voles— and larger prey like jackrabbits, ground squirrels, prairie dogs, and marmots. They also eat snakes, lizards, birds, and large insects. Golden Eagles are capable of killing very large animals like foxes, young deer, lambs, and even coyotes, but that does not happen very often. Carrion is another important food source, and Golden Eagles often follow scavengers like crows and vultures to feeding sites.

HABITAT & RANGE

Golden Eagles live in many different places throughout the West from high in the mountains to deep in the desert. They are rare in the East. For nesting, a pair selects a high, secluded cliff or tall tree in which to build its large stick nest. Most eagles in the United States don't

DESPITE its broad wings, a Golden Eagle can quickly **change** direction and speed when it sees something edible down below.

A CLOSER LOOK

Adults are dark brown.

Adult

Pointed feathers on the head and neck are tinged with gold.

Unlike most other hawks and eagles, its legs are feathered, not bare.

Large eyes can spot prey from a great distance. A ridge of bone over the eyes protects them from the wind or a struggling animal.

Heavy hooked bill for tearing flesh and skin

Bright yellow toes with large, sharp talons are used for grabbing prey.

migrate; they live in the same area all year. Some that nest in the far north migrate south for the winter. Golden Eagles also live in Europe and Asia.

RANGE MAP KEY

SUMMER (breeding)		WINTER (nonbreeding)	
MIGRATION		YEAR-ROUND	

HUMAN IMPACT

Last century, Bald Eagles were dying out because they ate fish that were full of pesticides that washed into the water from farm fields. The poisonous chemicals caused Bald Eagles to lay eggs with very thin shells that broke when they were being incubated. Luckily, Golden Eagles don't eat much fish; they eat small, pesticide-free mammals and escaped the harm done to Bald Eagles. But other human activities threaten Golden Eagles. The construction of huge wind turbines in wilderness areas has led to collisions that have killed eagles; rural power poles often carry live wires that can electrocute them when the large birds' wings or feet make contact with two lines and form an electrical circuit; and even though there are laws protecting all eagles, some sheep ranchers still shoot and poison them, believing that the eagles are killing their lambs.

Steller's Jay

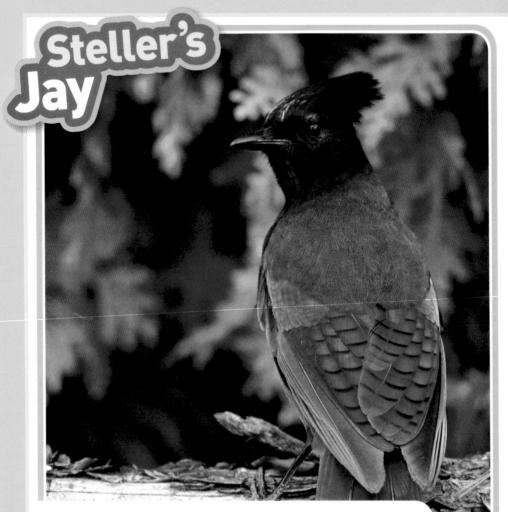

THE STELLER'S JAY is a large, turquoise, dark blue, and black bird with a shaggy-edged crest that lives in many western locations. These jays are especially common in mountain pine forests. Like other jays, Steller's are loud, bold, and curious, interacting with people in backyards, parks, and campgrounds. They fly on broad wings, interspersing flapping with gliding, and make a lot of noise with their harsh, scolding calls. In wilder places and especially when nesting they can be very shy. In the fall and winter, they form small flocks and cooperate with each other. A "sentry" bird will stand guard, alert for any danger, while the others in the flock forage quietly, knowing that their backs are covered.

SCIENTIFIC NAME: *Cyanocitta stelleri*
LENGTH: 11½ in (29 cm)
WINGSPAN: 19 in (48 cm)

VOICE

Steller's Jays have a variety of calls that include a piercing *SHECK-SHECK-SHECK* and a harsh, *JEAAHHH.* Other sounds include a variety of rattles and whistles. Skillful mimics, Steller's Jays often imitate the sounds that other birds and animals make. The most common imitation is the screaming call of a Red-tailed Hawk, but they also mimic squirrel calls, barking dogs, and chickens.

FOOD

In the wild, Steller's Jays eat insects, small animals, seeds, berries, and nuts; and sometimes other birds' eggs and nestlings. They feed in trees and on the ground. In picnic areas and camp-grounds they eat anything they can steal or convince people to offer to them. They are easily attracted to backyard bird feeders.

HABITAT & RANGE

Steller's Jays live in tall-timber country—usually evergreens or evergreens mixed with deciduous trees like oaks—from sea level to high in the mountains. Their nest is a cup of twigs and leaves with an inner lining of grass situated high in a tree on a horizontal limb. Though Steller's Jays do not usually migrate, they sometimes move to lower elevations in winter. These birds also live in Mexico and Central America.

STELLER'S JAYS can glide down from the treetops by simply opening and closing their **short wings.**

A CLOSER LOOK

Long blackish crest. The only other jay with a crest is the Blue Jay, which lives in the East.

Vivid blue wings with fine black barring

Long tail helps to maneuver when flying in tight spaces.

Most birds have blue lines on the head; birds from the southern Rockies have white lines.

Powerful bill handles varied foods, from acorns to lizards.

RANGE MAP KEY

WINTER (nonbreeding)   YEAR-ROUND

CACHING AND CASHING IN

Steller's Jays hide acorns and pine nuts to eat later when there is less food available (caching). They have excellent memories and can remember where hundreds of different food stashes are located. They also are sneak thieves. If one jay sees another taking a nut off to be stashed, it watches from a distance and, after the other bird leaves, moves in for the heist. These jays also know that "it takes a thief to know a thief." If a jay notices another jay watching, it waits until it's sure that the other bird is gone before it hides its prize nut.

Mountain Bluebird

A SMALL MEMBER of the thrush family, the Mountain Bluebird nests high in the mountains and also lives in open areas and ranchland in the American West. Males are a dreamy sky blue color and the female is cloaked in soft brownish gray. When spring arrives, the male claims a nest hole and defends it from rival males. Suitable nest holes can be hard to find, and he needs a good location in order to attract a female to mate with. Inside the cavity, the female does most of the nest building, weaving together a cozy nest cup of weed stems, grass, and pine needles and lining it with feathers, moss, and hair. She lays five to six pale blue eggs and sits on them for about two weeks before they hatch.

SCIENTIFIC NAME: *Sialia currucoides*
LENGTH: 7¼ in (18 cm)
WINGSPAN: 14 in (36 cm)

VOICE

The Mountain Bluebird's song is a series of short, warbled notes, *tru-lee tru-lee*, and its call is a thin, nasal-sounding *few*.

FOOD

Bluebirds are insect eaters. In the summer, their diet consists mostly of beetles, grasshoppers, crickets, caterpillars, ants, and bees. Their usual hunting method is dropping down from a perch to catch an insect on the ground, but they also catch bugs on the fly and hover over grasslands searching for prey. During the winter, they supplement their insect diet with fruit and berries.

HABITAT & RANGE

During summer, Mountain Bluebirds prefer open country with some trees, usually at high elevations—from 5,000 up to 12,000 feet. They nest in old woodpecker holes and other cavities and also use birdhouses. For the winter months, Mountain Bluebirds move to lower elevations. Small flocks congregate to forage in open woodlands or over grasslands and alfalfa fields. Seeing a winter flock of these

THE female Mountain Bluebird is actually brownish **gray** with just a hint of blue on her wings.

A CLOSER LOOK

Very long wings allow it to hover briefly while searching for insects on the ground.

Powder blue belly and slightly darker blue above

Female

Male

Fine-tipped bill is perfect for catching small insects.

sky blue birds hovering over a field is a very special experience. Birds nesting in Canada and Alaska migrate south in the fall. In the Rockies, birds move to slower elevations in fall, and sometimes they stray to the East Coast in winter.

RANGE MAP KEY

SUMMER (breeding)	WINTER (nonbreeding)
MIGRATION	YEAR-ROUND

I'M OUTTA HERE

Young bluebirds—and many other kinds of birds—are often anxious to leave their nest or birdhouse, even before they can fly. Maybe it gets cramped in there or maybe they just know that it's safer outside. Snakes and raccoons often try to raid bluebird nests. The young birds' spotted plumage is good camouflage if they have to hop around on the ground for a few days before getting airborne. They also have very loud begging calls, so their parents will know where they are and feed them.

Western Tanager

VIVIDLY BEAUTIFUL, the male Western Tanager has a black-and-yellow body and a bright red head. They show quite a bit of variation in the amount of red coloring on the head due to their unique way of obtaining pigment—they eat it! Western Tanagers do not manufacture the red pigment the way other tanagers do; it comes from insects the birds eat during breeding season. Imagine if you ate a diet of cherry Popsicles and your hair turned red.

During migration and in winter, males mostly eat fruit and lose the red color of their heads. Brightly colored Western Tanagers can be surprisingly difficult to find when they are feeding on insects high up in the trees. But seeing your first one through binoculars is something you'll never forget.

SCIENTIFIC NAME: *Piranga ludoviciana*
LENGTH: 7¼ in (18 cm)
WINGSPAN: 11½ in (29 cm)

VOICE

Western Tanagers have been described as having a short, burry song that sounds "like a robin with a sore throat." Their call is a piercing *pit-er-ICK!*

FOOD

Caterpillars, bees, wasps, beetles, grasshoppers, termites, and cicadas are just some of the insects that make up the Western Tanager's diet. They often feed in the treetops, moving slowly from branch to branch, picking insects off of the vegetation. Flying insects are sometimes caught on the wing, and flowers are searched for insects that might be hidden inside a blossom, attracted to the nectar. Berries and some cultivated fruit are also eaten, especially in winter.

HABITAT & RANGE

Western Tanagers breed in the high mountains in evergreen or aspen forests, sometimes in the far north. During migration, they occur in every habitat in the West, even the desert. A few Western Tanagers spend the winter in California

THE FEMALE Western Tanager is dressed in very different colors than the male. She is **olive gray** and greenish yellow.

A CLOSER LOOK

Winter male

Fairly heavy bill for dealing with caterpillars and cutting open fruit

Upper wing bar is yellow, lower wing bar is white.

Bright red and yellow colors of the male are unmistakable.

Summer male

Plump body and short black tail

eucalyptus groves, but most fly south to their winter homes in Mexico and Central America.

RANGE MAP KEY

SUMMER (breeding)	WINTER (nonbreeding)
MIGRATION	

GROWING UP FAST ... REALLY FAST

There's nothing unusual about the way baby Western Tanagers grow up; in fact, many songbirds have very similar life histories. After the female lays her three to five eggs, she sits on them (incubates them) for about 13 days until they hatch. Both parents feed the nestlings a diet of insects. The nestlings grow their first coat of feathers in about 10 to 14 days. At this point they can fly, and leave the nest, never to return. (Nests are actually dangerous places because of the predators that eat eggs and baby birds, so leaving fast is a good thing.) The parents feed the young birds and shepherd them around the neighborhood for about two more weeks. That's it, from hatching to college graduate in about a month!

Mini-Profiles

WESTERN MOUNTAINS

The famous national parks in the Rockies are great places to look for birds that love forests of evergreens and aspens. Next time you're at a park or anywhere else outdoors in the Rockies area, keep your eyes peeled for these birds.

The White-throated Swift is one of the fastest flying birds in North America and spends the entire day in the air pursuing flying insects. Its plumage is black with a white throat and a white line down the belly. Flying birds have thin, swept-back wings and hold their long tails in a point. In the Rockies, White-throated Swifts cruise high above steep-walled canyons and river gorges. In southern and central California, they fly above coastal cliffs and are seen soaring over cities. Nests are located in cliff crevices and holes in canyon walls. The saucer-like nest is made of weed stems, grass, and feathers, all glued together with the swift's sticky saliva.

WHITE-TAILED PTARMIGAN

SCIENTIFIC NAME: *Lagopus leucura*
LENGTH: 12½ in (32 cm)
WINGSPAN: 22 in (56 cm)

White-tailed Ptarmigans (TAR-meh-gehns, with a silent "p") are tame, chickenlike birds that like cold weather. During the summer, if the temperature gets above 70°F they go looking for a snowbank to cool off in. These small members of the grouse family are masters of camouflage. In winter their plumage is snowy white, and in summer they grow a whole new set of mottled brown feathers that make them look just like rocks. Adults are vegetarians, feeding on the buds and leaves of low-growing alpine plants. Very young chicks consume a protein-rich diet of insects.

BROAD-TAILED HUMMINGBIRD

SCIENTIFIC NAME: *Selasphorus platycercus*
LENGTH: 4 in (10 cm)
WINGSPAN: 5¼ in (13 cm)

Broad-tailed Hummingbirds nest at high elevations in the central and southern Rocky Mountains, where they feed on the nectar of abundant wildflowers and swarm around hummingbird feeders when they can. The male has a rose red throat; the female's throat is white with green spots. This tiny bird is well adapted to survival in the mountains, where nights can be cold even during the summer. It can enter a body state called torpor, lowering its body temperature and slowing its heart rate to save enough calories to survive the night. The female does all of the nest building, incubates the eggs, and feeds the two nestlings.

WHITE-THROATED SWIFT

SCIENTIFIC NAME: *Aeronautes saxatalis*
LENGTH: 6½ in (17 cm)
WINGSPAN: 15 in (38 cm)

CLARK'S NUTCRACKER

SCIENTIFIC NAME: *Nucifraga columbiana*
LENGTH: 12 in (31 cm)
WINGSPAN: 24 in (61 cm)

The Clark's Nutcracker is a crowlike, mountain bird with a gray body, black wings and tail, and a patch of white under the tail. This noisy bird is often heard before it is seen. Its call is loud and drawn out—a harsh, grating *KRA-A-A*. Although nutcrackers live high in the mountains and far from people, these bold bird are often encountered at scenic overlooks along mountain roads and in picnic areas and campgrounds looking for a handout. They normally depend on pine nuts (conifer seeds) for their main food. During summer and fall, the birds harvest thousands of seeds and store them in hidden caches. Remarkably, the birds remember where almost all of the hiding places are.

VIOLET-GREEN SWALLOW

SCIENTIFIC NAME: *Tachycineta thalassina*
LENGTH: 5¼ in (13 cm)
WINGSPAN: 13½ in (34 cm)

The colorful Violet-green Swallow has a moss green back and head, and a rump tinged with glossy violet. Its pure white underparts and face sometimes cause it to be confused with the White-throated Swift (see opposite page), but it has broader wings and flies with slower, fluttery wing beats. Like other swallows, the Violet-green feeds on flying insects. During the summer months, it is common to see small flocks flying over pine forests in the Rocky Mountains and other western locations all the way to Alaska. They nest in tree cavities, holes in cliffs, and even in birdhouses. As summer draws to a close, Violet-green Swallows migrate to their winter home in Mexico.

AMERICAN DIPPER

SCIENTIFIC NAME: *Cinclus mexicanus*
LENGTH: 7½ in (19 cm)
WINGSPAN: 11 in (28 cm)

The American Dipper draws gasps of admiration not because of its fine feathers, but because of its surprising lifestyle. Other birds live along the same rushing western streams, but only the dipper jumps into the icy water and walks underwater to search for food. Fighting the tricky currents, it picks larvae (the immature stage of an insect) from rocks and catches small minnows. This pudgy gray bird never strays far from the rushing water and sometimes builds its nest behind a small waterfall. Although many dippers live in the Rocky Mountains, they are found all the way from Alaska to Central America.

SNOWY OWL

Rock Star
Birds

Rock Star Birds of North America

The big, noisy Trumpeter Swan flaps its long wings up to Alaska each spring, to nest on the marshy edges of ponds and lakes. Winters are spent not very far south, on ice-free lakes and rivers in the northern U.S. and western Canada. Swans form pair bonds when they are three or four years old and stay together throughout the year, migrating in the same flock, often for a lifetime, which can last more than 20 years. Trumpeter Swans were hunted almost to extinction by the late 1800s, because their long flight feathers made the finest quill pens.

WHOOPING CRANE

SCIENTIFIC NAME: *Grus americana*
LENGTH: 52 in (132 cm)
WINGSPAN: 87 in (221 cm)

Because of habitat loss, the Whooping Crane—the tallest bird in North America—almost went extinct in the 1940s, when only 16 birds were left alive. Thanks to the efforts of conservationists in the U.S. and Canada, there are about 600 Whooping Cranes alive today. It remains an endangered species, breeding in northern Canada and wintering on the Texas Gulf Coast. One captive-breeding program teaches young birds their migration route by leading them with ultralight aircraft.

TRUMPETER SWAN

SCIENTIFIC NAME: *Cygnus buccinator*
LENGTH: 60 in (152 cm)
WINGSPAN: 80 in (203 cm)

ROSEATE SPOONBILL

SCIENTIFIC NAME: *Platalea ajaja*
LENGTH: 32 in (81 cm)
WINGSPAN: 50 in (127 cm)

Because of the Roseate Spoonbill's bright pink color, first-time observers in southern Florida and along the Gulf Coast often think they're seeing a flamingo. Take a closer look and you'll see the differences. The spoonbill has a wide flattened bill, bald greenish head, and shorter legs. To feed, the spoonbill swings its spoon-shaped bill from side to side until it feels a small fish or other tasty morsel. Like other large waterbirds, the spoonbill was hunted almost to extinction during the late 19th century for its beautiful feathers, which were used to decorate women's hats.

CALIFORNIA CONDOR

SCIENTIFIC NAME: *Gymnogyps californianus*
LENGTH: 47 in (119 cm)
WINGSPAN: 108 in (274 cm)

This huge, carrion-eating vulture is the largest flying bird in North America, with a wingspan of up to nine feet. Once common from Baja to the Canadian border, the condor was driven to the point of extinction. In 1987, the last nine birds—all living in the mountains of southern California—were caught and put into a captive-breeding program at the San Diego Wild Animal Park and Los Angeles Zoo. In recent years, young captive-bred California Condors have been released into wilderness areas in California, Arizona's Grand Canyon, Utah's Zion National Park, and the mountains of Baja California, Mexico.

ATLANTIC PUFFIN

SCIENTIFIC NAME: *Fratercula arctica*
LENGTH: 12½ in (32 cm)
WINGSPAN: 21 in (53 cm)

Puffins look like penguins wearing clown masks, with their black-and-white bodies and huge, multicolored bills. They aren't penguins, they are members of a family of seabirds called auks. Unlike penguins, the puffin's wings allow it to fly in the air as well as under the water. (Penguins only use their wings under water. They can't fly.) Atlantic Puffins breed on rocky islands off the coast of Maine and farther north, and spend winters at sea in the North Atlantic. The puffin has the ability to hold up to a dozen slippery, eel-like fish in its bill at one time.

SNOWY OWL

SCIENTIFIC NAME: *Bubo scandiacus*
LENGTH: 23 in (58 cm)
WINGSPAN: 52 in (132 cm)

Known as the "ghost hunter of the North," a Snowy Owl played a prominent role in the Harry Potter series as Hedwig, Harry's messenger owl. Some Snowy Owls live in their Arctic tundra home all year long, while others migrate south in winter to southern Canada, New England, New York, and the northern plains states, and in some years can be found in the Midwest and Pacific Northwest. Unlike most owls, Snowy Owls hunt during the day, which can last 24 hours during the Arctic summer. Their main food is a small rodent called a lemming, and a single bird can eat more than 1,600 lemmings in a year.

International Rock Star Birds

OSTRICH

SCIENTIFIC NAME: *Struthio camelus*
LENGTH: 96 in (244 cm)
WEIGHT: up to 320 lbs (145 kg)—flightless

The Ostrich—the world's largest living bird—is taller than a human adult and lives in Africa. It can't fly, but that's not a problem, as it can run at more than 40 miles an hour across open ground. Contrary to popular belief, the Ostrich does not bury its head in the sand, but often lies down with its head on the ground when hiding from a predator, such as a lion. If it's threatened, it kicks out with its powerful legs and fistlike feet, a deadly combination.

EMPEROR PENGUIN

SCIENTIFIC NAME: *Aptenodytes forsteri*
LENGTH: 38 in (97 cm)
WEIGHT: up to 100 lbs (45 kg)—flightless

All of the world's 17 species of penguin live in the Southern Hemisphere. The Emperor Penguin, which lives in Antarctica, is the biggest. All penguins are flightless, but Emperor Penguins walk as much as 125 miles inland from their fishing grounds to gather in huge breeding colonies every year. Each pair lays a single egg. The male incubates it—on his feet!—for two months in winter weather that can go down to 60° below zero F and has nothing to eat for the entire time. The female walks back to the coast to feed and trades off parenting duties with the male after the egg has hatched.

WANDERING ALBATROSS

SCIENTIFIC NAME: *Diomedea exulans*
LENGTH: 50 in (127 cm)
WINGSPAN: 132 in (335 cm)

Superstitious sailors believe that seeing an albatross is good luck, but killing one will curse their ship and everyone aboard. The Wandering Albatross is an awe-inspiring bird. It has the longest wingspan—almost 11 feet from tip to tip—and is the most powerful flyer of all the world's seabirds. Some individuals are known to fly 100,000 miles a year without ever touching land—that's almost halfway to the moon! Young birds spend up to ten years at sea, until they are mature enough to mate and raise a family—one chick every other year—on remote ocean islands.

HARPY EAGLE

SCIENTIFIC NAME: *Harpia harpyja*
LENGTH: 42 in (107 cm)
WINGSPAN: 80 in (203 cm)

The Harpy Eagle lives in the Neotropical rain forest and is the largest and most powerful eagle in the world. It flies through the forest—expertly dodging tree trunks and branches—on massive wings, hunting medium-size mammals. Its prey is snatched up by its powerful legs and feet and carried off held in its eight massive talons. Monkeys and anteaters are frequent prey, but its favorite food is the tree-dwelling sloth, which can weigh up to 20 pounds, about the same weight as the Harpy Eagle itself.

KEEL-BILLED TOUCAN

SCIENTIFIC NAME: *Ramphastos sulfuratus*
LENGTH: 28 in (71 cm)
WINGSPAN: 50 in (127 cm)

A huge colorful bill makes the toucan easy to identify. Toucans live in the New World tropics where their huge bills allow them to reach fruits at the end of branches too skinny to support their weight. These bills are used to explore tree cavities looking for frogs, lizards, and other things to eat. The bill looks heavy, but is actually very light and strong, and is covered with a layer of keratin, the very same biological material that your fingernails are made of. Keel-billed Toucans live in lowland forests from southern Mexico to Venezuela.

RESPLENDENT QUETZAL

SCIENTIFIC NAME: *Pharomachrus mocinno*
LENGTH: 14 in (36 cm), plus 24 in (61 cm) for male's plumes. **WINGSPAN:** 22 in (55 cm)

The Resplendent Quetzal (pronounced KET-zawl) is the most beautiful bird in the Western Hemisphere. The male has long, trailing plumes up to two feet long, which twist and dance when he flies, giving him a magical quality in the air. Quetzals primarily eat fruit—wild avocado is a favorite—which is swallowed whole. Later on, the seed is regurgitated (spit up) in a different place and sometime sprouts, thus producing a new tree and eventually more food for the quetzal.

How to Build a Bird Feeder

SODA BOTTLE BIRD FEEDER

Feeding birds is fun. If you hang a bird feeder near a window, you can look out and see an amazing parade of beautiful birds. It's easy to make your own bird feeder, and it doesn't cost a lot. The birds will like it just as much as an expensive store-bought one. During the winter months when food is scarce, the seed you provide may help the birds survive. When it's warm out, the birds can find their own food, but you can still feed them if you want to. You can find birdseed for your feeder at most grocery, hardware, and pet stores. Mixed birdseed will do the job and is not expensive, but the best seed for wild birds is black-oil sunflower seed, which doesn't cost much more.

MATERIALS YOU WILL NEED

- 1 two-liter plastic soda (or water) bottle
- Ruler
- Marker
- Utility knife
- 2 wooden spoons
- 1 small screw eye
- Twine for hanging
- Birdseed
- Funnel

1 Remove the outside wrapper from the plastic bottle, rinse the bottle well, and turn it upside down to dry.

2 With a ruler, measure 2 inches up from the bottom and use the marker to draw a ½-inch "X" to mark the spot. Then, turn the bottle 90 degrees and measure 5 inches up

162

from the bottom and draw another $\frac{1}{2}$-inch "X" to mark the spot. Then draw a 1-inch-wide circle opposite both of the X-marks, as shown.

3 This next step is a parent or guardian's job. Ask an adult to use the utility knife to slit the two X-marks and cut out the 1-inch circles.

4 Insert a wooden spoon handle through each of the cutout circles and then push handles through the X-mark. The wooden spoons will act as a perch and also catch seed that falls out.

5 The first part of this step is also a parent or guardian's job. Ask an adult to remove the cap and use the utility knife to poke a small hole in the top of it. Then you can take the screw eye and twist it into the center of the top. Next, attach a piece of twine to the screw eye and tie it tightly in a knot. The length of the twine will depend on the height of the branch or bird feeder hanger you want to hang the feeder from. You may want to take the twine and hang it from the branch or hanger to see how far down you would like your feeder to be.

6 Now you're almost done. Fill your feeder with birdseed—use the funnel to pour the seed into the small opening. Before you put the cap back on, hang it from the tree first. The easiest way to hang the bird feeder is to use a slipknot. Then screw your bird feeder on. You may need an adult to help you. Now you're done! Sit back, relax, and enjoy all of the wonderful birds you will see!

NOTE: Location is important! Hang your feeder far enough away from bushes so that a hungry cat can't reach it in a single pounce. If you want to watch the feeder from inside, hang it near a window, but make sure it is no more than a foot away from the glass. If it's farther away, a bird that is scared off can fly full speed into the window glass and hurt itself.

How to Make a Birdbath

Birds don't need anything fancy or complicated, just a shallow pool of water to drink and splash in—they'll use a puddle in the road, if they find one.

A simple birdbath can be set up using three flowerpots and a plant saucer—the kind that goes under a potted plant. It can be made of clay or plastic, depending on what you prefer.

MATERIALS YOU WILL NEED
• **Three clay flowerpots,** with diameters that differ by two inches (one 12", one 14", and one 16", for example)

• **One clay plant saucer.** Make sure the saucer is at least a few inches wider than the bottom of your smallest flowerpot so it is big enough for the birds to enjoy!

• **Water-based clear gloss paint sealant** (this item should be used only by a grown-up).

• **Acrylic paints in assorted colors.** Make sure the paints you buy are weather resistant. Patio paint is a good option.

• **Paintbrushes**

• **Super glue** (this item should be used only by a grown-up).

MAKING YOUR BIRDBATH
1. Stack your flowerpots upside down with the largest one on the bottom, the medium size one in the middle, and the smallest one on top.

2. Mark dots around the rim of each flowerpot with a pencil so you know which parts of the pots will be covered.

3. Ask an adult to seal the inside of each pot and the saucer with two or three coats of the water-based sealant. Allow the sealant to dry(placing the items in the sun will help them to dry quickly). Ask a grown-up to make sure the pots and saucer are completely dry.

4. Once the pots are completely dry, start painting! Use your imagination and be creative!

5. Once you are done painting, let your birdbath dry completely.

ASSEMBLING YOUR BIRDBATH

1. The first step must be done by a grown-up: Use the super glue to glue the bottom of the plant saucer to the bottom of the smallest flowerpot.

2. Let the saucer and small flowerpot dry completely. It is best if you allow it to dry overnight.

3. When the saucer and small pot are dry, choose a location for your birdbath and take all materials to that location to start putting your birdbath together.

4. Once you have the perfect location, turn the largest flowerpot upside down and place the medium-size flowerpot on top of it, upside down. Then place the small flowerpot, with saucer attached, on top of the medium pot, also upside down.

5. Your birdbath is now complete! All you have to do is add some water and enjoy the bird-watching!

Be sure to change the water every three or four days, and clean the birdbath, especially the saucer, weekly to prevent algae or bacteria from growing.

NOTE: Instead of clay pots, you can buy sturdy, weather-resistant plastic flowerpots and saucer. If you buy plastic you may want to purchase them in different colors or with different patterns for variety. Then you can follow instructions under "Assembling Your Birdbath."

How to Build a Bird Nest

Many bird species use the materials they find near their nesting areas to weave a shelter where they can lay their eggs, keep the eggs safe and warm until they hatch, and then protect and feed their nestlings until they can fly on their own two wings. If you have ever found a bird's nest and looked at it closely, you were probably amazed at the way the bird wove together natural materials to form a cozy cup or a basket of sticks. Now you can build one of your own!

MATERIALS YOU WILL NEED

- **A plastic tarp** or large plastic bag
- **Scissors**
- **A paper bag**
- **Colored construction paper**
- **A cereal bowl** for the nest mold
- **Plastic wrap**
- **School glue**
- **2 small paper cups**
- **Water**
- **A bowl** for the glue and water mixture
- **A plastic spoon**
- **Feathers and moss** (You can find these at a craft store.)

PUTTING YOUR BIRD NEST TOGETHER

1. Set up a plastic tarp or large plastic bag to use as your surface for making the nest. Place all materials on the tarp or bag.

2. Cut the paper bag and the colored construction paper into strips about ½-inch thick and put them aside.

3. Cover the outside of your cereal bowl with plastic wrap (this is to ensure the nest won't stick to the bowl when it's dry).

4. Pour about 3 ounces of glue into one of the small paper cups and 3 ounces of water into the other. Then pour both into your mixing bowl.

5. Use the plastic spoon to stir the glue and water together until they are completely mixed.

6. Dip your strips of paper one by one into the mixture and start placing them on top of the cereal bowl.

7. Keep layering until the entire bowl is covered, then repeat until you have covered the bowl in two or three layers of paper. Use as many colors as you like and make sure to layer the paper at different angles.

8. Every now and then, gently smooth the strips down.

9. When you're done, allow this to dry for about 24 hours.

10. When the nest is completely dry, carefully remove the nest from the plastic surface, and then carefully remove the plastic wrap from the nest. You should now have a lovely bird nest!

11. Carefully glue your feathers and moss inside the nest (birds often use different materials to line their nest to keep eggs and babies warm).

12. Your bird nest is now complete!

Drawing birds can be easy and fun, once you learn a few basic steps. Looking closely at a bird in order to draw it is a great way to learn more about it. You can also look at photos or paintings of birds. Start with blank white paper, a sharp #2 pencil, and a good eraser. You can add color later with colored pencils or watercolors. Don't press too hard with your pencil at the start. It'll be easier to erase when you want to.

1. DRAW THE BASIC SHAPES

Start with two ovals—a large one for the body and a smaller one for the head. Some birds have large heads and others have small ones, compared to the size of their bodies. At the rear end, a wedge shape connects the tail to the body. How long is the tail, compared to the body? Add lines close together under the body oval if you want the bird's feet to have a branch to perch on.

2. IMPROVE THE SHAPE OF THE BIRD

Add slightly curved lines at the throat and the back of the head to connect the head and body. Erase the inside lines where the two circles meet; they are no longer needed. Add a shape for the bill and a small circle for the eye—the eyes usually are close to the bill, not in the center of the head. Draw a slightly stretched-out oval for the folded wing. Draw the legs where they come out of the body toward the branch (or the ground, if you are

drawing a standing bird instead of a perching one). Erase any lines that you no longer need, and darken the ones that you want to keep.

3. ADD DETAILS

Keep working on the shapes, and start to add feather details in the wings and tail. When working on the wings, pay attention to how the feathers overlap. Add details to the bill and draw the feet gripping the branch (or on the ground).

4. ADD PATTERNS AND SHADING

When the shape and feather outlines of the bird are done, you can draw in the light and dark patterns of the bird. Use light pressure with the side of the pencil's tip for lighter areas and heavier pressure with the pencil tip for darker areas or stripes. If the bird is colorful, use your colored pencils or watercolors.

5. IDENTIFY THE BIRD

Write the name of the bird on your drawing, and the date that you drew it. It's lots of fun to go back later to see the drawings you've done in the past!

6 Things You Can Do to Help Birds

1. KEEP CATS INDOORS

Every year, cats kill millions of wild birds. Pet cats do not have to go outside to hunt in order to have a good life. Some people think that putting a small bell around a cat's neck will warn birds and protect them, but this does not work.

2. PREVENT PICTURE-WINDOW COLLISIONS

Windows are among the major killers of wild birds. Sometimes, a big pane of glass can reflect the outdoors like a mirror. Birds can't tell that the glass is there and they fly right into it. Some birds are killed instantly by the impact. Others are merely stunned and will be able to fly away after a brief recovery, though some of those will die later from their injuries. If you have a big window or glass door that birds have crashed into, break up the reflections by covering the outside with decals, or hang suncatchers, crystals, or feathers, which work best if they sway in the wind. These must be close together over the entire surface of the glass in order to work.

3. FEED BIRDS IN YOUR YARD OR ON YOUR BALCONY

In parts of the country where winters are cold, birds sometimes struggle to find enough food when the temperature drops or snow covers the ground. Putting up bird feeders, or even scattering birdseed on the ground, greatly helps the birds that are living near you year-round. If you can, put up a suet feeder, available in many pet supply stores. Or make a peanut butter pinecone: Spread natural peanut butter on a pinecone and then roll it in unsalted sunflower seeds or peanuts. Try to hang it up where the squirrels can't get to it! Keep feeders clean.

4. SAFELY DISCARD PLASTIC BAGS AND SIX-PACK HOLDERS

Birds who scavenge in landfills and dumps—especially gulls—can be injured or killed by getting their heads caught in the plastic loops that hold soda cans together. Before you throw them away or recycle them, take a pair of scissors and snip open every loop. Tie knots in plastic bags before you discard them, so that birds don't get trapped in them.

5. AVOID CHEMICAL PESTICIDES AS MUCH AS POSSIBLE

Insects are essential to the survival of many species of birds. Don't use chemical insect foggers in your yard, and switch to natural, nontoxic methods of pest control for garden plants and flowers. Support farmers who are committed to growing food without using toxic chemicals by eating sustainably grown food as much as you can.

6. BECOME A "CITIZEN SCIENTIST" IN YOUR OWN HOME

Project Feeder Watch, sponsored by Cornell University, is a great way to help birds, and everyone is welcome to participate. You identify and count birds coming to your feeder and transmit your data online—it becomes part of a huge database that helps scientists and conservationists who work to protect birds. For more information, check out the Project Feeder Watch website: *www.birds.cornell.edu/pfw*.

Glossary

bill: The tough, outside covering of a bird's jaw. Bills (or beaks) come in all shapes and sizes, usually adapted to what the bird feeds on. Bills are made of the same material as a person's fingernails.

breeding plumage: For those birds with two plumages a year, the breeding plumage (or summer plumage) is worn when a bird is courting or nesting, usually in the spring and summer. *(See winter plumage.)*

call: Bird sounds that are generally shorter than songs and made by both males and females. Calls convey a specific message. Unlike songs, calls are not learned; each bird is born knowing the unique calls that its species makes. *(See song.)*

colony: A group of birds that nest close together

egg: The way all birds reproduce. The tiny embryo is nourished by the attached food supply (the yolk) and surrounded by a cushion of watery gel (the white); the whole thing is enclosed in a hard calcium case (the eggshell).

estuary: A river mouth with tidal mudflats that provide a rich feeding ground for many birds

extinct bird: A species of bird that no longer exists anywhere in the world

feather: Feathers are unique to birds. They grow from the skin and emerge rolled up in a thin tube (pin feather). Different types of feathers serve different functions, from strong wing feathers for flight to soft, downy feathers for insulation.

flock: A group of birds; can be of all the same species, or a mixed flock made up of different species.

hybrid: An unusual bird that is the result of breeding between two individuals of different species

immature: Not fully adult. For some birds, such as the Bald Eagle, it takes four to five years to reach adult plumage. Some immature birds are capable of breeding.

incubation: Maintaining the eggs at an even temperature, usually in a nest, until they hatch

juvenile: A young bird wearing its first coat of feathers (not the down it hatches in). A bird grows to its full adult size within the first year of life. Although full-grown, a juvenile can still look different from an adult because its feathers have different colors or patterns. *(See immature.)*

migration: The regular movement of birds to and from an area. In North America, *spring migration* is usually the northbound movement of birds to their breeding grounds; *fall migration* is the southbound movement of birds to the area where they spend the winter. Many species do not migrate.

molt: The replacement of old feathers with new ones. Most species replace all of their feathers once a year, but they do it slowly over a period of weeks or months.

ornithologist: A scientist who studies birds

plumage: Term for all the feathers that cover a bird's body

preening: Feather maintenance behavior, in which a bird grasps a feather near its base, then nibbles along the shaft towards the tip. This action cleans and smooths the feather.

primary feathers: The long and sturdy feathers of the outer part of the wing that make flight possible

roost: To sleep, or the place where a bird sleeps

scientific name: The unique, two-part name that scientists agree on for every plant and animal. The names are derived from Greek or Latin.

song: A pattern of notes usually sung by a male bird (sometimes a female) to attract a mate or defend a territory. Most young birds learn their song by copying an adult. *(See call.)*

songbird: A type of bird with a complex voice box that can sing more complex songs than other birds

tail feathers: Most birds have 12 tail feathers, although it varies. These feathers assist in flight, and are especially useful in making quick turns.

waterfowl: Ducks, geese, and swans

wing bars: One or two colored bars (often white) that run across a bird's wing

winter plumage: Many birds only have one plumage—they look the same all year. For those birds with two plumages a year, the winter plumage (or nonbreeding plumage) is worn when the bird is not courting or nesting, usually in the fall and winter. *(See breeding plumage.)*

Find Out More

To learn more about birds and stay connected to young birders around the country, check out these books, movies, and websites.

BOOKS
Hiaasen, Carl. *Hoot.* Yearling, 2005

Hoose, Phillip. *Moonbird: A Year on the Wind with the Great Survivor.* Farrar, Straus, and Giroux, 2012

Koch, Maryjo. *Bird Egg Feather Nest.* Smithmark, 1999

MOVIES AND DVDS
BBC Video. "The Life of Birds" (NR documentary)

Questar. "Hummingbirds: Magic in the Air" (NR documentary)

Sony Pictures. *Winged Migration* (rated G)

Warner Brothers. *March of the Penguins* (rated G)

WEBSITES
All About Birds (The Cornell Lab of Ornithology): www.allaboutbirds.org

Backyard Birding (National Geographic): www.nationalgeographic.com/animals/birding

Just for Kids (National Audubon Society): www.audubon.org/educate/kids

KidWings: www.kidwings.com

Index

Photo Credits

Abbreviations: GI = Getty Images; NGMS = National Geographic My Shot; SS = Shutterstock

FRONT COVER: blue jay, All Canada Photos/GI; hummingbird, Chesapeake Images/SS; bird house, Galchenkova Ludmila/SS; nest and eggs, D&D Photos/SS; eagle, Steve Collender/SS; **BACK COVER:** binoculars, Andrei Shumskiy/SS; western tanager, Richard Cronberg/ NGMS; mute swan, Jim Nelson/NGMS; **INSIDE FRONT AND BACK COVER ILLUSTRATIONS:** Jonathan Alderfer; David Beadle; Peter Burke; Marc R. Hanson; Cynthia J. House; H. Jon Janosik; Donald L. Malick; John P. O'Neill; Kent Pendleton; Diane Pierce; John C. Pitcher; H. Douglas Pratt; David Quinn; N. John Schmitt; Thomas R. Schultz; Daniel S. Smith; **FRONT MATTER:** 2-3, Delpho/ARCO/ naturepl.com; 4 (LE), Geoff Powell/NGMS; 4 (RT), Thy Bun/NGMS; 5 (LE), George Quiroga/NGMS; 5 (RT), Gallo Images/GI; 6, Bill Dodsworth/NGMS; 9, Akihiro Asami/NGMS; 12, Rohan Kulkarni/NGMS; 13 (LE), All Canada Photos/GI; 13 (RT), Stuart Clarke/NGMS; **EASTERN BACKYARD:** 14, Robin Loznak/NGMS; 14, John Warburton-Lee/AWL Images RM/GI; 15 (LE), James Cumming/NGMS; 15 (RT), Pam Morris/NGMS; 16-17, Robin Loznak/NGMS; 16 (UP), All Canada Photos RM/GI; 18 (UPLE), Steven Russell Smith Photos/SS; 18 (UPRT), L F File/SS; 18 (CTR), Arindam Bhattacharya/NGMS; 18 (LO), Steve Brigman/SS; 19 (UPLE), p.schwarz/SS; 19 (UPRT), Al Mueller/SS; 19 (CTR), Joey Bamburg/NGMS; 19 (LORT), Gerald Marella/SS; 19 (LOLE), Jim Ridley/NGMS; 19 (LOCTR), Kassia Halteman/SS; 20, Joey Bamburg/NGMS; 21 (UP), Michelle Earle/NGMS; 21 (CTR), H. Douglas Pratt; 21 (LO), Bill Telzerow/NGMS; 22, Jim Mullins/NGMS; 23 (UP), Sharon and Mike Tobin/NGMS; 23 (CTR), H. Douglas Pratt; 23 (LO), Thomas Voyd/NGMS; 24, Nuwan Ganganath/National Geographic Stock; 25 (UP), Julia Martin/NGMS; 25 (CTR), H. Douglas Pratt; 25 (LO), Roman Zhitenev/NGMS; 26, Jim Ridley/NGMS; 27 (UP), Pam Morris/NGMS; 27 (CTR), Diane Pierce; 27 (LO), William Mullins/Alamy; 28 (UP), p.schwarz/SS; 28 (CTR), Steven Russell Smith Photos/SS; 28 (LO), Steve Brigman/SS; 29 (UP), Gerald Marella/SS; 29 (CTR), Al Mueller/SS; 29, Kassia Halteman/SS; **WESTERN BACKYARD:** 30-31, Guang Chow/NGMS; 32-33 (BACK), David Madison/GI; 32 (LE), Thy Bun/NGMS; 32 (RT), Gavin Emmons/NGMS; 33 (UPLE), Alejandro Herrera/NGMS; 33 (UPRT), michael ohaion/NGMS; 33 (LE CTR), Tommy Sherrell/NGMS; 33 (UP CTR), Steve & Dave Maslowski/GI; 33 (RT CTR), Stuart Clarke/NGMS; 33 (LOLE), Mickey Samuni/NGMS; 33 (LOCTR), Shonn Morris/NGMS; 33 (LORT), May Woon/NGMS; 34, Brian Griffith/NGMS; 35 (UP), Paul Marto/NGMS; 35 (CTR), H. Douglas Pratt; 35 (LO), Thy Bun/NGMS; 36, Christopher Corman/NGMS; 37 (UP), Mark Zukowski/NGMS; 37 (CTR), Donald L. Malick; 37 (LO), Gavin Emmons/NGMS; 38, Quentin Furrow/NGMS; 39 (UP), May Woon/NGMS; 39 (CTR), H. Douglas Pratt; 39 (LO), May Woon/NGMS; 40, Lee F. Snyder/GI; 41 (UP), SaraJo/SS; 41 (CTR), H. Douglas Pratt; 41 (LO), Rolf Nussbaumer Photography/Alamy, 42 (UP), Michael Ohaion/NGMS; 42 (CTR), Kathrine Lloyd/NGMS; 42 (LO), Mickey Samuni/NGMS; 43 (UP), Steve & Dave Maslowski/GI; 43 (CTR), H. Douglas Pratt; 43 (LO), Shonn Morris/NGMS; **CITY STREETS AND PARKS:** 44-45, Uri Rosenberg/NGMS; 46-47 (BACK), Walter Bibikow/GI; 46 (UPLE), Christine Haines/NGMS; 46 (UPRT), Mario Tizon/NGMS; 46 (CTR), Joseph Rescinito/NGMS; 46 (LO), Steve and Dave Maslowski/GI; 47 (UPLE), Akihiro Asami/NGMS; 47 (UPRT), Mary Ann Bridge/NGMS; 47 (LE CTR), Rohan Kulkarni/NGMS; 47 (LOLE), Jamie Link/NGMS; 47 (LOLE), Kristin Renbarger/NGMS; 47 (LORT), Beverly Cochran/NGMS; 48, Akihiro Asami/NGMS; 49 (UP), Patrick Lanham/NGMS; 49 (CTR), Donald L. Malick; 49 (LO), Luc Henri Fage/NGMS; 50, Ron Storey/NGMS; 51 (UP), Gerome Dennie/NGMS; 51 (CTR), H. Douglas Pratt; 51 (LO), Mary Ann Bridge/NGMS; 52, Joseph Rescinito/NGMS; 53 (UP), Kathrine Lloyd/NGMS; 53 (CTR), H. Douglas Pratt; 53 (LO), Christina Quackenbush/NGMS; 54, Christine Haines/NGMS; 55 (UP), Elliott Neep/GI; 55 (CTR), N. John Schmitt; 55 (LO), Uri Rosenberg/NGMS; 56 (UP), Kristin Renbarger/NGMS; 56 (CTR), Mario Tizon/NGMS; 56 (LO), Jamie Link/NGMS; 57 (UP), Steve and Dave Maslowski/GI; 57 (CTR), Beverly Cochran/NGMS; 57 (LO), Toni Chowdhury/NGMS; **FARMS AND FIELDS:** 58-59, Mikael Johansson/NGMS; 60-61 (BACK), Shobeir Ansari/Flickr Open/GI; 60 (UPRT), Richard Cronberg/ NGMS; 60 (LO), Flickr Open/GI; 60 (LO), Linda Moore/NGMS; 60 (UPLE), Jim Zipp/GI; 61 (UPLE), Larry Keller/NGMS; 61 (UP CTR), Marcus Armani/NGMS; 61 (UPRT), Vince Maidens/NGMS; 61 (CTR), Jim Nelson/NGMS; 61 (LOLE), James Cumming/NGMS; 61 (LORT), Philip Haber/NGMS; 62, Vince Maidens/NGMS; 63 (UP), Alex Thomson/NGMS; 63 (CTR), Donald L. Malick; 63 (LO), Konrad Wothe/Minden Pictures; 64, Jim Zipp/GI; 65 (UP), Boguslaw Brzyski/NGMS; 65 (LE), N. John Schmitt; 65 (LO), Ron Storey/NGMS; 66, Cissy Beasley/ NGMS; 67 (UP), Jan Galland/NGMS; 67 (CTR), H. Douglas Pratt; 67 (LO), Akihiro Asami/NGMS; 68, Raymond Barlow/NGMS; 69 (UP), janet furlong/NGMS; 69 (CTR), H. Douglas Pratt; 69 (LO), Larry Keller/NGMS; 69 (LO), Richard Cronberg/NGMS; 70 (UP), James Cumming/ NGMS; 70 (CTR), Jim Nelson/NGMS; 70 (LO), Marcus Armani/NGMS; 71 (UP), Flickr Open/GI; 71 (C R), Linda Moore/NGMS; **BEACH AND BAY:** 74-73, Jeff Maurtizen/National Geographic; 74-75, Tim Fitzharris/Minden Pictures; 74 (UP), Mary Ann Bridge/NGMS; 74 (LE CTR),

Bill Beckner/NGMS; 74 (RT CTR), Dinuk Magammana/NGMS; 74 (LO), Kristine Lat/NGMS; 75 (UP CTR), Vijayanand CD/NGMS; 75 (UPLE), Joseph Straccia/NGMS; 75 (CTR), Jeff Mauritzen/National Geographic Stock; 75 (UPRT), Linh Dinh/NGMS; 75 (LOLE), Andrea Lypka/NGMS; 75 (LORT), Aravind Krishnaswamy/NGMS; 76, Jeff Mauritzen/National Geographic Stock; 77 (UP), Dwight Sokoll/NGMS; 77 (CTR), Jonathan Alderfer; 77 (LO), Jeff Mauritzen/National Geographic Stock; 78, Warren Sharpp/NGMS; 79 (UP), Steve Ellwood/NGMS; 79 (CTR), Donald L. Malick; 79 (LO), Michael Wulf/NGMS; 80, Daboost/SS; 81 (UP), Vijayanand CD/NGMS; 81 (CTR), Thomas R. Schultz; 81 (LO), Paul J Fusco/GI; 82, Tom Helinski/NGMS; 83 (UP), Boris Hristev/NGMS; 83 (CTR), Thomas R. Schultz; 83 (LO), Jim Gray/NGMS; 84 (UP), Kristine Lat/NGMS; 84 (CTR), Joseph Straccia/NGMS; 84 (LO), Aravind Krishnaswamy/NGMS; 85 (UP), Sunita Budhrani/NGMS; 85 (CTR), Per Smitterberg/NGMS; 85 (LO), Bill Beckner/NGMS; **SOUTHERN SWAMP AND BAYOU:** 86-87, Mike Delgado/NGMS; 88-89 (BACK), Gallo Images/Danita Delimont/GI; 88 (UP), Visuals Unlimited, Inc./John Cornell/GI; 88 (LO), Teresa Darragh/NGMS; 88 (CTR), Mark Lewer/NGMS; 89 (LE CTR), Hideta Nagai/NGMS; 89 (UPLE), Michael Nichols/National Geographic Creative/GI; 89 (UPRT), Terry Piotraschke/NGMS; 89 (RT CTR), Thomas LeClair/NGMS; 89 (CTR), Vladimir Kalinovsky/NGMS; 89 (LOLE), Steve Ellwood/NGMS; 89 (LORT), Steve Gettle/Minden Pictures; 90, Kris Docken/NGMS; 91 (UP), Phil Reid/SS; 91 (CTR), Diane Pierce; 91 (LO), Thomas LeClair/NGMS; 92, Terry Piotraschke/NGMS; 93 (UP), Francoise Macomber/NGMS; 93 (CTR), H. Jon Janosik; 93 (LO), Savannah Whitwam/NGMS; 94, Derek Dafoe/NGMS; 95 (UP), Michael Nichols/National Geographic Creative/GI; 95 (CTR), Donald L. Malick; 95 (LO), Michael Nichols/National Geographic Creative/GI; 96, Steve Gettle/Minden Pictures; 96 (UP), Scott Leslie/Minden Pictures; 96 (CTR), Cynthia J. House; 96 (LO), Nathan Lovas Photography; 98 (UP), Vladimir Kalinovsky/NGMS; 98 (CTR), Teresa Darragh/NGMS; 98 (LO), Visuals Unlimited, Inc./John Cornell/GI; 99 (UP), Steve Ellwood/NGMS; 99 (CTR), Hideta Nagai/NGMS; 99, Mark Lewer/NGMS; **RIVER AND MARSH:** 100-101, Sandor Bernath/NGMS; 102-103 (BACK), Raymond Gehman/National Geographic Creative/GI; 102 (UPLE), Brian Dawson/NGMS; 102 (UPRT), pix2go/SS; 102 (LO), George Whalen/NGMS; 103 (UPLE), Mike DeBonis/NGMS; 103 (UPRT), Raymond Barlow/NGMS; 103 (LE CTR), Edward Mattis/NGMS; 103 (RT CTR), Nick Chill/NGMS; 103 (LOLE), Sandor Bernath/NGMS; 103 (LOCTR), Gregory Johnston/SS; 103 (LORT), Chuh Hung Kao/NGMS; 104, Randy Rimland/SS; 105 (UP), Harlan Humphrey/NGMS; 105 (CTR), Diane Pierce; 105 (LO), John Sutton/NGMS; 106, Bruce Leonard/iStockphoto; 107 (UP), John Starsja/NGMS; 107 (CTR), Donald L. Malick; 107 (LO), Yoshikatsu Nagaya/NGMS; 108, Steve Ellwood/NGMS; 109 (UP), Ike Austin/NGMS; 109 (CTR), Donald L. Malick; 109 (LO), Monika Petersen/NGMS; 110, Glenn Young/SS; 110 (UP), Dennis Gazso/NGMS; 111 (UP), Steve Creek/NGMS; 111 (CTR), H. Douglas Pratt; 111 (LO), Edward Mattis/NGMS; 112 (LO), Tony Britton/NGMS; 112 (CTR), Dave Karnes/NGMS; 113 (LO), Sandor Bernath/NGMS; 113 (UP), Martin Knippel/NGMS; 113 (CTR), Cosmin Nahaiciuc/NGMS; **PRAIRIE AND PLAINS:** 114-115, Steven Smith/NGMS; 116-117, Kellie L. Folkerts/SS; 116 (UP), John Stankewitz/NGMS; 116 (CTR), CR Courson/Flickr RF/GI; 116, Noelle Zaleski/NGMS; 117 (UPLE), Donald M. Jones/Minden Pictures; 117 (UP CTR), Mike Kuran/NGMS; 117 (UPRT), Steve & Dave Maslowski/GI; 117 (LE CTR), Tim Zurowski/GI; 117 (RT CTR), Wim Weenink/Minden Pictures; 117 (LORT), William H Mullins/GI; 117 (LORT), Gary Meszaros/GI; 118, Graham Owen/NGMS; 119 (UP), Stubblefield Photography/SS; 119 (CTR), Donald L. Malick; 119 (LO), Marcus Armani/NGMS; 120, All Canada Photos/Alamy; 121 (UP), John Stankewitz/NGMS; 121 (CTR), Jonathan Alderfer; 121 (LO), Jim Zipp/GI; 122, Stephen Dalton/Minden Pictures; 123 (UP), Dietmar Nill/NGMS; 123 (CTR), H. Douglas Pratt; 123 (LO), Wim Weenink/Minden Pictures; 124, Photo Researchers/GI; 125 (UP), Wayne Lynch/GI; 125 (CTR), Thomas R. Schultz; 125 (LO), Rolf Nussbaumer/NPL/Minden Pictures; 126 (LO), photographer/Minden Pictures; 126 (CTR), Noelle Zaleski/NGMS; 127 (CTR), Marcel van Kammen/Foto Natura/Minden Pictures; 127 (LO), Markus Varesvuo/NPL/Minden Pictures; 127 (UP), John Stankewitz/NGMS; **DESERTS:** 128-129, William Leaman/Alamy; 130-131, Paul B. Moore/SS; 130 (UP), Nasim Mansurov/NGMS; 130 (CTR), All Canada Photos/Alamy; 130 (LO), SuperStock/Alamy; 131 (UPLE), Owen Newman/GI; 131 (UP CTR), Angel Di Bilio/NGMS; 131 (UPRT), Stubblefield Photography/SS; 131 (CTR), Cissy Beasley/NGMS; 131 (LOLE), Anton Foltin/SS; 131 (LOCTR), Danita Delimont/GI; 131 (LORT), Alexander Viduetsky/NGMS; 132, Tom Vezo/Minden Pictures; 133 (UP), Cyril Ruoso/JH Editorial/Minden Pictures; 133 (CTR), N. John Schmitt; 133 (LO), Rolf Nussbaumer/NPL/Minden Pictures; 134, David Tipling/NPL/Minden Pictures; 135 (UP), Konrad Wothe/Minden Pictures; 135 (CTR), H. Douglas Pratt; 135 (LO), Danita Delimont/GI; 136, Tom Vezo/Minden Pictures; 137 (UP), Jim Zipp/GI; 137 (CTR), Donald L. Malick; 137 (LO), Owen Newman/GI; 138, Jared Hobbs/GI; 139 (UP), Walter Meayers Edwards/National Geographic Creative/GI; 139 (CTR), H. Douglas Pratt; 139 (LO), Nature/UIG/GI; 140 (UP), SuperStock/Alamy; 140 (CTR), Anton Foltin/SS; 140, All Canada Photos/Alamy; 141 (UP), Angel Di Bilio/NGMS; 141 (CTR), Cissy Beasley/NGMS; 141 (LO), Stubblefield Photography/SS; **WESTERN MOUNTAINS:** 142-143, Konrad Wothe/Minden Pictures; 144-145 (BACK), Rudy Balasko/SS; 144 (UPLE), Tom Vezo/Minden Pictures; 144 (UPRT), Glen Bartley/GI; 144 (LO), Ernest Ross/NGMS; 145 (UPLE), Werner Bollmann/GI; 145 (UPRT), Enrique Rabelo/NGMS; 145 (LE CTR), Scot Heath/NGMS; 145 (UP CTR), Dena Miller/NGMS; 145 (RT CTR), Jack Milchanowski/Visuals Unlimited, Inc./GI; 145 (LOLE), Catherine Ashbee/NGMS; 145 (LORT), Jeff Brubaker/NGMS; 146, Raymond Barlow/NGMS; 147 (UP), Guy Edwardes/GI; 147 (CTR), Donald L. Malick; 147 (LO), David Madison/GI; 148, Tom Vezo/Minden Pictures; 149 (UP), Roy H. Photography/Flickr RF/GI; 149 (CTR), H. Douglas Pratt; 149 (LO), Larsen Calvin/GI; 150, Dena Miller/NGMS; 151 (UP), Walter Nussbaumer/NGMS; 151 (CTR), H. Douglas Pratt; 151 (LO), Tom Vezo/Minden Pictures; 152, Bob Smith/National Geographic Creative/GI; 153 (UP), Catherine Ashbee/NGMS; 153 (CTR), Jack Milchanowski/Visuals Unlimited, Inc./GI; 153 (CTR), Peter Burke; 153 (LO), Glen Bartley/GI; 153 (UP), Charles Melton/Alamy; 153 (LO), Bob Cochran/NGMS; 155 (UP), Scot Heath/NGMS; 155 (CTR), Julie Callison/NGMS; 155 (LO), Enrique Rabelo/NGMS; **ROCK STAR BIRDS:** 156-157, Vince Maidens/NGMS; 156 (UPRT), Bill Dodsworth/NGMS; 156 (LO), Ryan Hoelke/NGMS; 156 (UPLE), Shane Rucker/NGMS; 157 (UP), Mike DeBonis/NGMS; 157 (CTR), Pierre Larouche/NGMS; 157 (LO), Robert Biondo/NGMS; 158 (UPRT), Jeff Mauritzen/National Geographic Stock; 158 (UPLE), Keith Szafranski/iStockphoto; 158 (LO), Marc Faucher/NGMS; 159 (UPLE), Gary Vestal/GI; 159 (RT), worldswildlifewonders/SS; 159 (LO), James Hale; 160 -165, Lori Epstein.

ACKNOWLEDGMENTS

I'd like to thank all of the editorial and design staff at National Geographic Kids Books for their expertise and guidance. Priyanka Lamichhane, my patient editor, was a pleasure to work with and skillfully kept the project on point and on schedule. My wife, Zora Margolis, gently guided me with editorial advice and made numerous suggestions that greatly improved the text. She leavened my writing with her wit and sense of language in ways that I would never have thought of on my own. Thank you.

—Jonathan Alderfer

Credits

PUBLISHED BY THE NATIONAL GEOGRAPHIC SOCIETY

John M. Fahey, *Chairman of the Board and Chief Executive Officer*
Timothy T. Kelly, *President*
Declan Moore, *Executive Vice President; President, Publishing and Travel*
Melina Gerosa Bellows, *Executive Vice President; Chief Creative Officer, Books, Kids, and Family*

PREPARED BY THE BOOK DIVISION

Hector Sierra, *Senior Vice President and General Manager*
Nancy Laties Feresten, *Senior Vice President, Kids Publishing and Media*
Jonathan Halling, *Design Director, Books and Children's Publishing*
Jay Sumner, *Director of Photography, Children's Publishing*
Jennifer Emmett, *Vice President, Editorial Director, Children's Books*
Eva Absher-Schantz, *Design Director, Kids Publishing and Media*
R. Gary Colbert, *Production Director*
Jennifer A. Thornton, *Director of Managing Editorial*

STAFF FOR THIS BOOK

Priyanka Lamichhane, *Project Editor*
Jim Hiscott, *Art Director*
Lori Epstein, *Senior Illustrations Editor*
Project Design Company, *Designers*
Carl Mehler, *Director of Maps*
Paul Lehman, *Principal*, Sven M. Dolling and Michael McNey, *Map Research and Production*
Grace Hill, Michael O'Connor, *Associate Managing Editors*
Joan Gossett, *Production Editor*
Ariane Szu-Tu, *Editorial Assistant*
Kathryn Robbins, *Associate Designer*
Hillary Moloney, *Illustrations Assistant*
Callie Broaddus, *Design Production Assistant*
Lewis R. Bassford, *Production Manager*
Susan Borke, *Legal and Business Affairs*

MANUFACTURING AND QUALITY MANAGEMENT

Phillip L. Schlosser, *Senior Vice President*
Chris Brown, *Vice President, NG Book Manufacturing*
George Bounelis, *Vice President, Production Services*
Nicole Elliott, Rachel Faulise, Robert L. Barr, *Managers*

Title Page: A Bald Eagle catches a fish with its talons.

CELEBRATING ‹125› YEARS

The National Geographic Society is one of the world's largest nonprofit scientific and educational organizations. Founded in 1888 to "increase and diffuse geographic knowledge," the Society's mission is to inspire people to care about the planet. It reaches more than 400 million people worldwide each month through its official journal, *National Geographic*, and other magazines; National Geographic Channel; television documentaries; music; radio; films; books; DVDs; maps; exhibitions; live events; school publishing programs; interactive media; and merchandise. National Geographic has funded more than 10,000 scientific research, conservation and exploration projects and supports an education program promoting geographic literacy.

For more information, please visit www.nationalgeographic.com, call 1-800-NGS LINE (647-5463), or write to the following address:
National Geographic Society
1145 17th Street N.W.
Washington, D.C. 20036-4688 U.S.A.

Visit us online at www.nationalgeographic.com/books

For librarians and teachers: www.ngchildrensbooks.org

More for kids from National Geographic:
kids.nationalgeographic.com

For information about special discounts for bulk purchases, please contact National Geographic Books Special Sales: ngspecsales@ngs.org

For rights or permissions inquiries, please contact National Geographic Books Subsidiary Rights: ngbookrights@ngs.org

Library of Congress Cataloging-in-Publication Data
Alderfer, Jonathan K.
  National Geographic kids bird guide of North America : the best birding book for kids from National Geographic's bird experts / by Jonathan Alderfer.
     pages cm
  Includes bibliographical references and index.
  Audience: Ages 8-12.
  ISBN 978-1-4263-1094-2 (pbk. : alk. paper) -- ISBN 978-1-4263-1095-9 (library binding : alk. paper)
  1. Birds--North America--Identification--Juvenile literature. I. National Geographic Society (U.S.) II. Title. III. Title: Kids bird guide of North America.
  QL715.A433 2013
  598.097--dc23
                                    2012028615
Printed in the United States of America
13/QGT-LPH/1

NATIONAL GEOGRAPHIC